MW00634405

100 THE ROUGH GUIDE TO THE BEST PLACES IN SCOTLAND

100 BEST PLACES IN SCOTLAND

DISTRIBUTION

UK, Ireland and Europe
Apa Publications (UK) Ltd; sales@roughguides.com

United States and Canada
Ingram Publisher Services; ips@ingramcontent.com

Australia and New Zealand
Booktopia; retailer@booktopia.com.au

Worldwide
Apa Publications (UK) Ltd; sales@roughguides.com

SPECIAL SALES, CONTENT LICENSING AND CO-PUBLISHING

Rough Guides can be purchased in bulk quantities at discounted prices. We can create special editions, personalized jackets and corporate imprints tailored to your needs. Email: sales@roughguides.com
roughguides.com

Printed in China

First Edition 2022

A catalogue record for this book is available from the British Library

HELP US UPDATE

We've gone to a lot of effort to ensure that this first edition of The Rough Guide to the 100 Best Places in Scotland is accurate and up-to-date. But if you feel we've got it wrong or left something out, we'd like to know.
Please send your comments with the subject line "Rough Guides 100 Best Places in Scotland" to mail@uk.roughguides.com. We'll credit all contributions and send a copy of the next edition (or any other Rough Guide if you prefer) for the very best emails.

THE ROUGH GUIDE TO THE
100 BEST PLACES IN SCOTLAND

Editor: Joanna Reeves
Picture Editor: Tom Smyth
Designer: Pradeep Thapliyal
Head of DTP and Pre-press: Katie Bennett
Head of Publishing: Kate Drynan

100 THE ROUGH GUIDE TO THE BEST PLACES IN SCOTLAND

V&A
MACKINTOSH
AT THE
WILLOW

INTRODUCTION

For many visitors Scotland's calling card is the strikingly handsome Edinburgh, with its castle, historic Old Town and Fringe festivals. But beyond the poster capital, a scattering of cities surprise and delight: Glasgow and its edgy social scene, Dundee with its burgeoning cultural credentials, the silver Granite City of Aberdeen. Smaller fishing villages and towns prove size doesn't always matter, from the traditional lobster shacks in Crail to the cobbled streets of Culross.

Spectacular landscapes abound in the rugged Highlands; the lochs, hills and forested glens of the Trossachs giving way to the raw wilderness of the Cairngorms. Off shore, a string of islands tempts visitors out to sea to explore Mull and smaller sister Iona, the whisky distilleries of Islay and Jura and, of course, Skye, the jewel in the Hebridean crown.

Elsewhere, we uncover the curious corners and unexpected sights of Scotland: a whimsical sculptural park in West Lothian, the ethereal Bridge to Nowhere above the waters off Dunbar, the time-capsule isle of Ulva. Whether you picnic beside puffins on Lunga or discover footprint-free beaches on Gigha, we hope our pick of the 100 best places in Scotland will inspire you to explore this diverse and dramatic country.

EDINBURGH AND THE LOTHIANS

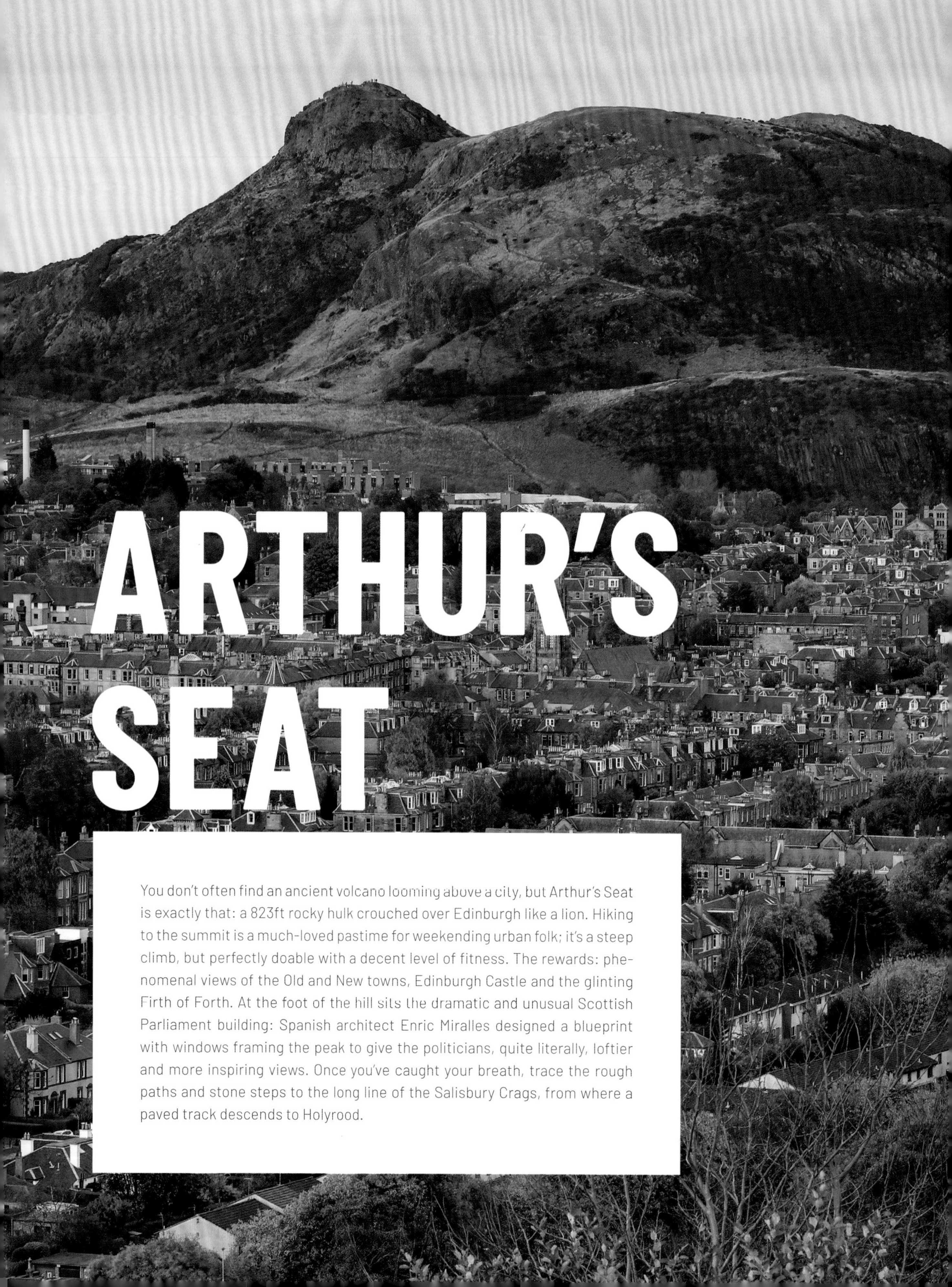

ARTHUR'S SEAT

You don't often find an ancient volcano looming above a city, but Arthur's Seat is exactly that: a 823ft rocky hulk crouched over Edinburgh like a lion. Hiking to the summit is a much-loved pastime for weekending urban folk; it's a steep climb, but perfectly doable with a decent level of fitness. The rewards: phenomenal views of the Old and New towns, Edinburgh Castle and the glinting Firth of Forth. At the foot of the hill sits the dramatic and unusual Scottish Parliament building: Spanish architect Enric Miralles designed a blueprint with windows framing the peak to give the politicians, quite literally, loftier and more inspiring views. Once you've caught your breath, trace the rough paths and stone steps to the long line of the Salisbury Crags, from where a paved track descends to Holyrood.

View of Holyrood Park and the Scottish Parliament from Salisbury Crags

Taking in the view from Arthur's Seat

The walk down from Arthur's Seat

Salisbury Crags from Calton Hill

Edinburgh Fringe hosts big names in music, theatre and comedy

The party continues late into the night during the Fringe

Silent disco tour during Edinburgh Festival Fringe

Pianodrome

ASSEMBLY ROOMS

Every August Scotland's capital shrugs off its refined air and embraces creativity through its world-leading cultural festivals. The Edinburgh International Festival was established in 1947 to celebrate diversity and the human spirit in the recovery from wartime, and focuses on theatre, classical music, opera and dance. The equally long-established Edinburgh Festival Fringe is a baggier and more anarchic affair: pubs, venues, front rooms and shops explode with arts events. If you're having problems navigating the 300-plus venues, then a visit to one of the Fringe big-hitters, the Assembly Rooms on George Street, is a good place to start. The building itself, with its Greek temple design, is one of the capital's grandest, which is saying something in this architectural hotbed. During the Fringe, an artsy crowd gathers here to catch acts by some of the biggest names in the music, theatre and comedy worlds. The party spills out onto the temporarily pedestrianized street and continues late into the night at impromptu beer gardens set up throughout the city.

The iconic Assembly Rooms

BRIDGE TO NOWHERE

There are few more arresting sights in Scotland than the Bridge to Nowhere, hovering serenely in the waters off Dunbar. Evocatively christened for its striking inundation at high tide, the bridge does in fact go somewhere, at least at low tide, when it connects the Biel Water and the beach at Belhaven Bay. When the waters rise around the bridge's steps, though, it's a brain-bending sight, beloved of photographers and locals alike. The distinctive Bass Rock, slumbering on the horizon like a giant turtle, lends an even more surreal edge to the scene. The site of the Jacobites' last stand on Scottish soil and a familiar location in the tales of Robert Louis Stevenson, the Rock today is home to the world's largest colony of northern gannets. Watch live feeds in peace from the Scottish Seabird Centre in nearby North Berwick or brace yourself for the cacophony of some 150,000 gannets on one of the centre's summer boat trips.

Duddingston Allotments

Duddingston Kirk

Herons, kingfishers and otters populate Duddingston Loch

Pink-footed geese at Duddingston Loch

Old Church Lane

DUDDINGSTON

Tucked into the lee of Arthur's Seat on the edge of a nature reserve, the sleepy village of Duddingston is a world apart from Edinburgh. The whole place – all two streets' worth – quietly marinates in Scottish history, with the Sheep Heid Inn laying fair claim to oldest pub (est. 1360) in the land. The clientele has included Mary, Queen of Scots, King James I and Bonnie Prince Charlie, with the latter holding a council of war just down the street at no. 8–10. Parallel to The Causeway is Old Church Lane, where a revelation of a secret garden lies sequestered behind high stone walls. Brought to life in the 1960s as a far sighted nature cure by husband-and-wife GPs, Dr Neil's Garden is a little slice of horticultural paradise filled with exotic trees and plants. Beguiling paths wend their way past Scots pine, Chilean araucaria (AKA monkey puzzle) and American sequoia down to the edge of Duddingston Loch, populated by herons, kingfishers and otters. Even in peak summer, the garden is rarely busy and you can sometimes have it all to yourself. When the sun shines and the light blinks off the water, you might be anywhere but rain-lashed Scotland.

Edinburgh Old Town from Calton Hill

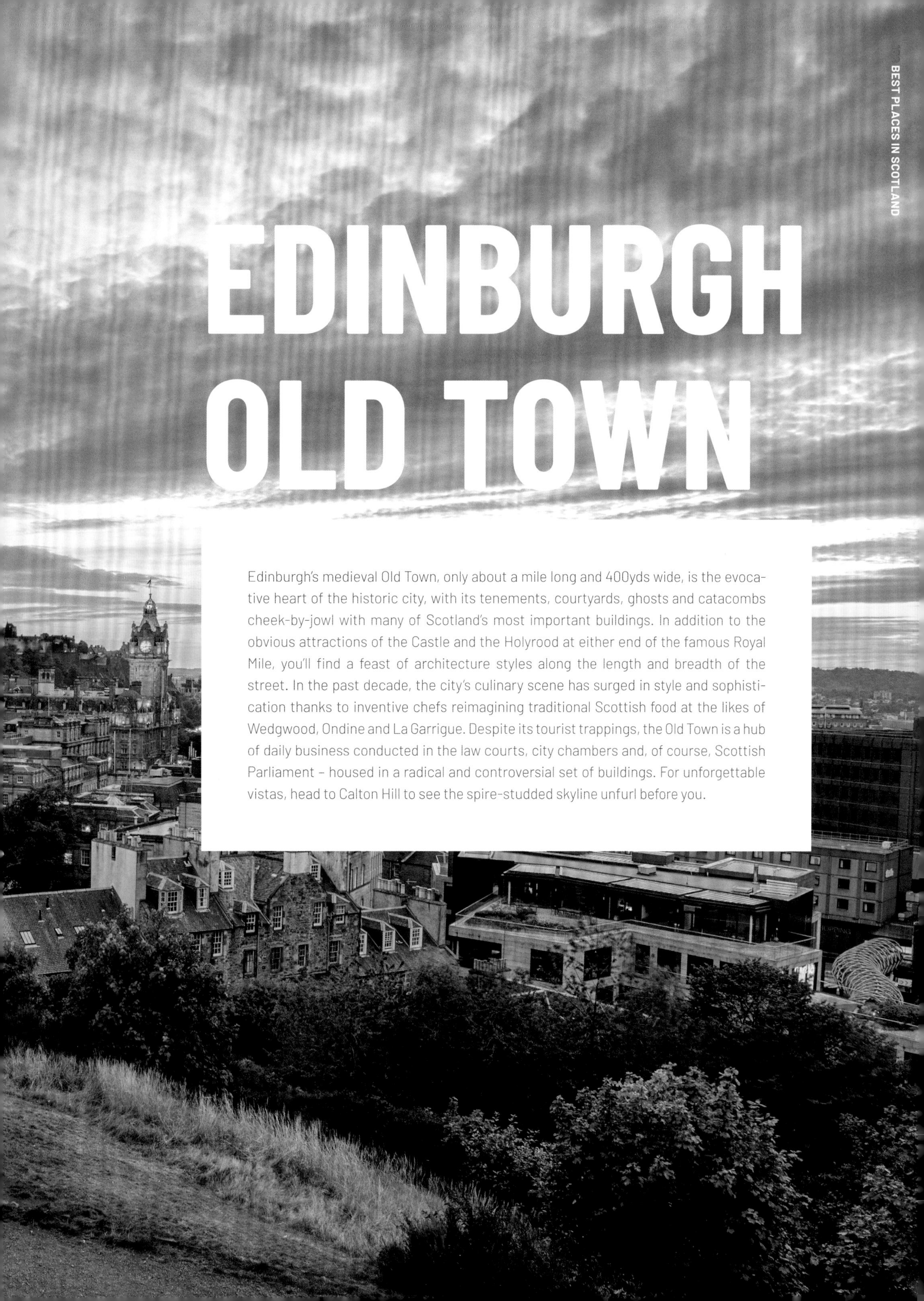

EDINBURGH OLD TOWN

Edinburgh's medieval Old Town, only about a mile long and 400yds wide, is the evocative heart of the historic city, with its tenements, courtyards, ghosts and catacombs cheek-by-jowl with many of Scotland's most important buildings. In addition to the obvious attractions of the Castle and the Holyrood at either end of the famous Royal Mile, you'll find a feast of architecture styles along the length and breadth of the street. In the past decade, the city's culinary scene has surged in style and sophistication thanks to inventive chefs reimagining traditional Scottish food at the likes of Wedgwood, Ondine and La Garrigue. Despite its tourist trappings, the Old Town is a hub of daily business conducted in the law courts, city chambers and, of course, Scottish Parliament – housed in a radical and controversial set of buildings. For unforgettable vistas, head to Calton Hill to see the spire-studded skyline unfurl before you.

Phyllida Barlow's first permanent artwork: *Quarry*

Rachel Maclean's dystopian funhouse, *Mimi*

Joana Vasconcelos' kaleidoscopic *Gateway*

Animitasa by Christian Boltanski

Nicolas Party: *Café Party*

JUPITER ARTLAND

Combining the best of contemporary and landscape art with the bucolic charms of a working country estate, Jupiter Artland makes for an enigmatic day-trip from Edinburgh. The brainchild of an art-collecting couple, the sculpture park sits in the 100-acre grounds of Bonnington House, 10 miles from the capital. Admirers of the late landscape designer Charles Jencks will instantly clock his trademark biospheric mounds at the entrance: the pristinely sculpted, cascading *Cells of Life* that flank the lake-dotted causeway. You likewise can't fail to miss Joana Vasconcelos' *Gateway*, a kaleidoscopic swimming pool made from over eleven thousand handmade Portuguese tiles. Explore further and you might discover Andy Goldsworthy's *Coppice Room* and its conspiratorial huddle of trees, or the darkly humorous, dystopian funhouse of Rachel Maclean's *Mimi*. The gorgeous Jacobean interiors of the galleries are as much as of a draw as the ever-changing exhibitions.

Linlithgow Palace at dusk

LINLITHGOW PALACE

Linlithgow Palace is a splendid fifteenth-century ruin romantically set on the edge of Linlithgow Loch. The pile is associated with some of Scotland's best-known historical figures, including Mary, Queen of Scots, who was born here on December 8, 1542 and became queen six days later. A royal manor house is believed to have existed on this site since the time of David I, though James I began construction of the present palace, a process that continued through two centuries and the reign of no fewer than eight monarchs. From the top of the northwest tower, Queen Margaret looked out in vain for the return of James IV from the field of Flodden in 1513 – indeed, the views from her bower, six giddy storeys up from the ground, are exceptional. The ornate octagonal fountain in the inner courtyard, with its wonderfully intricate figures and medallion heads, flowed with wine for the wedding of James V and Mary of Guise. The galleried Great Hall is magnificent, as is the adjoining kitchen.

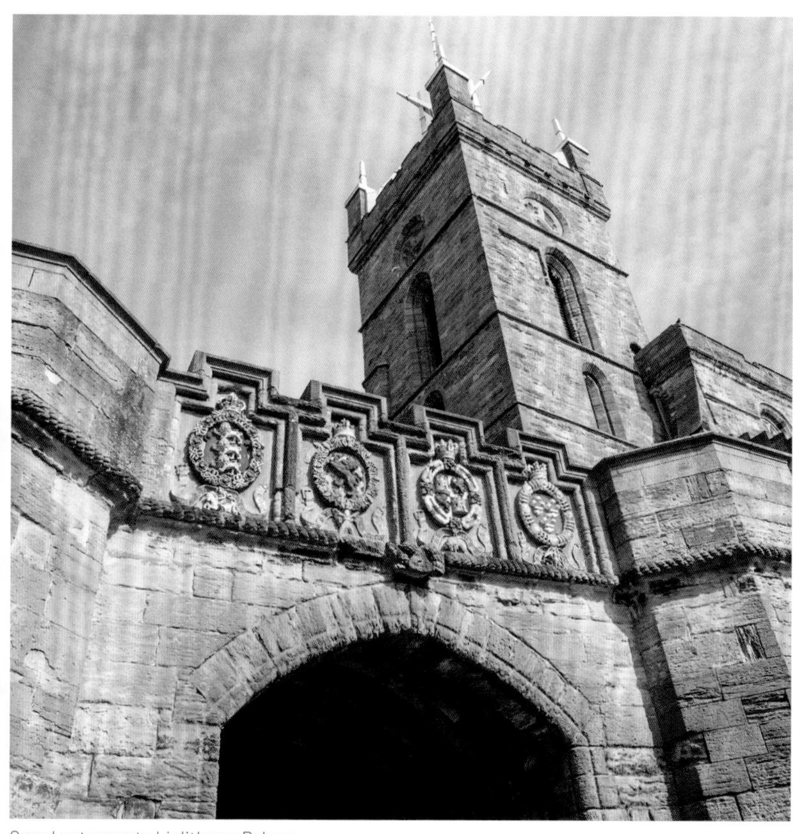
Grand entrance to Linlithgow Palace

Linlithgow Loch

Unicorn adorning the ornate fountain

Statue of Mary, Queen of Scots

The cylindrical tower of the new wing

NATIONAL MUSEUM OF SCOTLAND

The National Museum of Scotland sits at the heart of Edinburgh, and is very much a place of two halves. There's a fantastical Victorian wing that packs in a bedazzling array of artefacts, covering natural history, world culture, geology and technology. One standout exhibit is the gruesome Millennium Clock Tower, a jumble of cogs, chains and wheels modelled in the form of a Gothic cathedral, with gargoyles and sinister-looking figurines representing characters from twentieth-century politics. The newer building – a bold sandstone addition fronted by a striking cylindrical tower – traces Scotland's history, from the earliest people to the Union of the Crowns, the Jacobite Rebellion, the Industrial Revolution and on to pop culture and contemporary politics. Key exhibits are the quirkily expressive Lewis chessmen, a silver picnic set made for Bonnie Prince Charlie and a life-size working model of a steam-driven Newcomen Atmospheric Engine.

The fantastical Victorian Wing

Fashion exhibits

World Cultures gallery

Life-sized skeleton of a Tyrannosaurus rex

Leering gargoyles above windows and doors

Stained-glass details adorn the chapel

Rosslyn Chapel: a Gothic masterpiece

Sublime stonework

Rosslyn Chapel in the snow

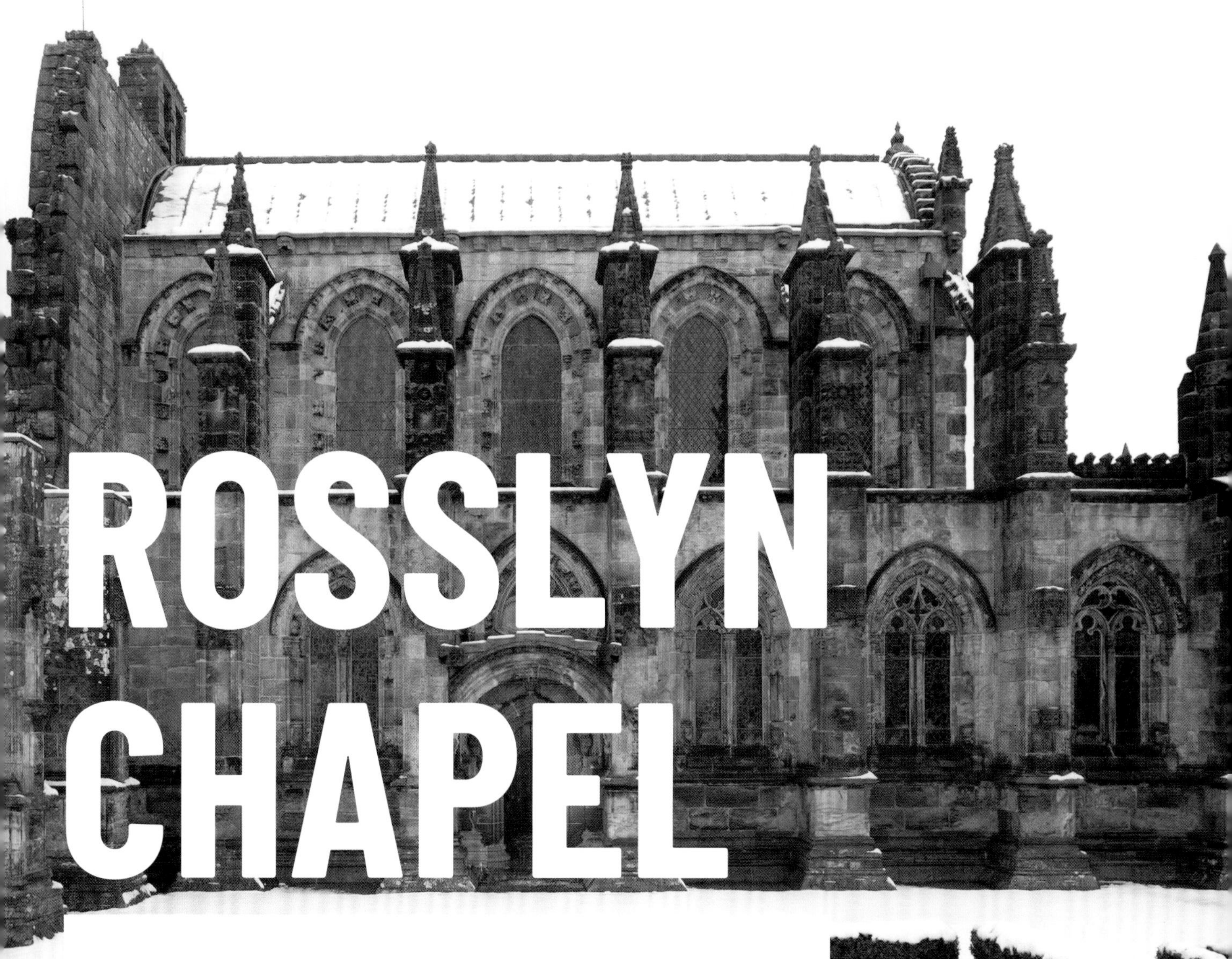

ROSSLYN CHAPEL

Sitting in hilly Midlothian south of Edinburgh, the fifteenth-century Rosslyn Chapel is revered for its sublime stone carvings - some of the finest in the world - and the subject of intrigue and mystery with its alleged Crusader connections. This richly decorated cathedral-like Gothic masterpiece is a testament to the skills of its medieval sculptors. Built in a highly ornate style, its exterior is a riot of flying buttresses, pinnacles and leering gargoyles - but it is the interior that fascinates with its stories etched in stone. First up, there are depictions of cacti and Indian corn that predate Columbus's 'discovery' of America. Secondly, there's the intricately knotted Apprentice Pillar, a work so dazzling that the jealous master allegedly killed his apprentice, whose figure - complete with violently slashed head - is scored into the ceiling. Thirdly, there are the Freemason and Knights Templar associations, signalled by carvings of a floriated cross and a five-point star, that have sparked the myth that the chapel houses the Holy Grail.

The gallery is filled with pre-twentieth-century European art

Martin Creed's art installation, *Everything is going to be alright*

A "temple to the fine arts"

Antony Gormley sculpture

SCOTTISH NATIONAL GALLERY OF MODERN ART

Built as a "temple to the fine arts" in 1850, the Scottish National Gallery houses the country's premier collection of pre-twentieth-century European art. Though by no means as vast as national collections found elsewhere in Europe, it does include some exquisite Old Masters and Impressionist works. Among the Gallery's most valuable treasures are Hugo van der Goes' *Trinity Panels*, on a long-term loan from the Queen. Poussin's *Seven Sacraments*, proudly displayed in their own room, mark the first attempt to portray scenes from the life of Jesus realistically, rather than through images dictated by artistic conventions. Among the canvases by Rembrandt is a poignant *Self-Portrait Aged 51*, while *Christ in the House of Martha and Mary* is the largest of the thirty or so surviving paintings by Vermeer. Gavin Hamilton's *Achilles Lamenting the Death of Patroclus* and Robert Burns' *The Hunt* are among the finer examples of Scottish art. One of the gallery's most popular portraits is the instantly recognizable painting of a lesser-known pastor, *Reverend Robert Walker Skating on Duddingston Loch*, by Henry Raeburn.

Nathan Coley artwork

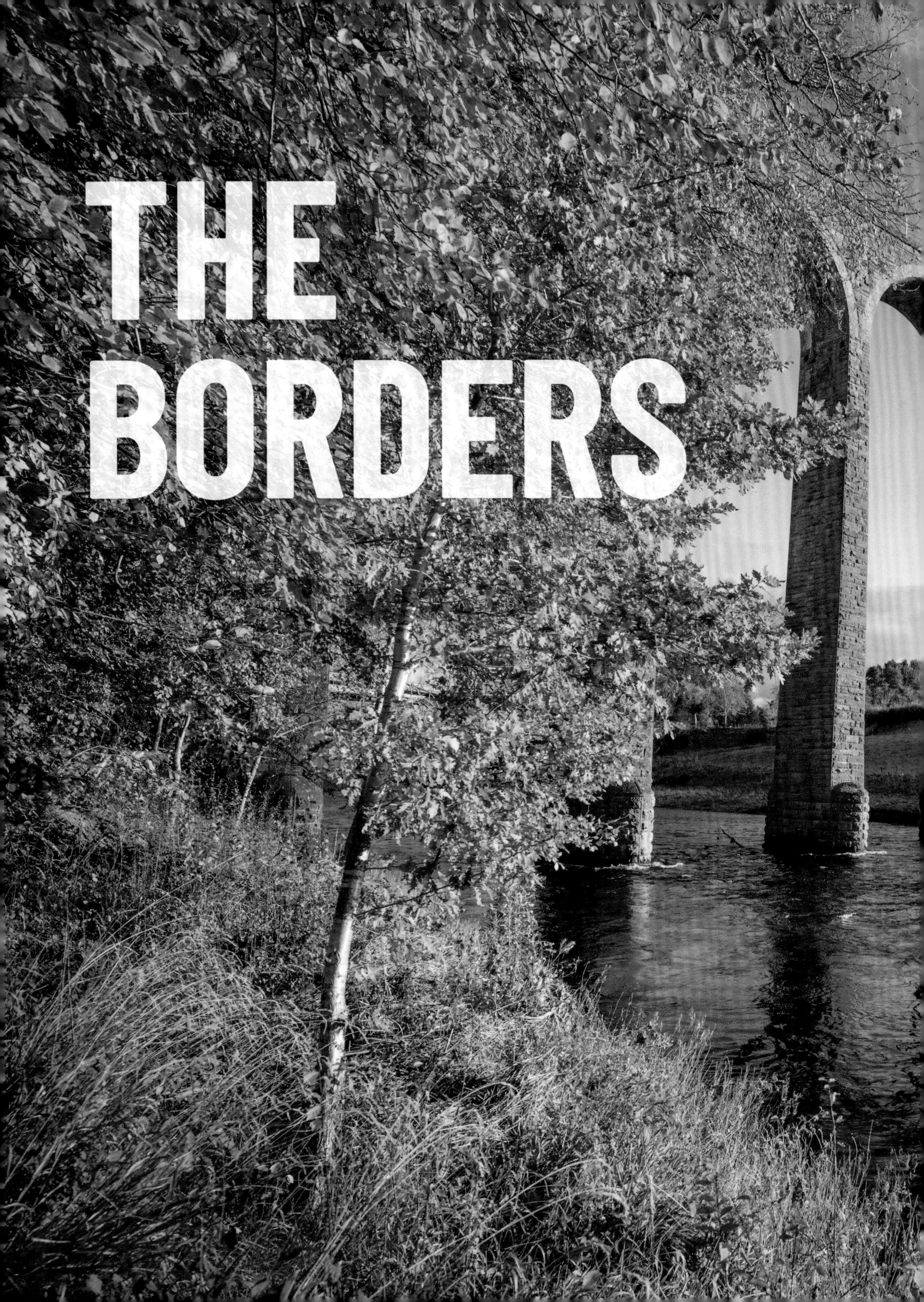

THE BORDERS

GLENTRESS FOREST

Glentress Forest has some of the best opportunities for mountain biking in Scotland. Not only are there five superb, carefully crafted, purpose-built trails – colour-coded for difficulty – there's a fantastic bike centre at the entrance to the forest called the Peel Gateway. This is a great place for bikers, with changing rooms and showers, a café and a shop filled with spares as well as bike rental from Alpine Bikes. If you fancy staying several days it's worth checking out the timber wigwams of Glentress Forest Lodges near the entrance. There are more adrenaline-pumping downhill trails through thick forest just a few miles southeast of Glentress near Innerleithen, geared towards more advanced riders, with bike rental available in Innerleithen. Glentress and Innerleithen combined are one of seven forest biking centres in southern Scotland, known collectively as the 7stanes.

Glentress Forest: one of Scotland's top biking destinations

Glentress Forest Lodges

Walking the paths

World-famous 7stanes mountain bike trails

Jedburgh: the best preserved of all the Border abbeys

A fine example of the transition from Romanesque to Gothic design

Tranquil abbey garden

Splendidly preserved stonework detail

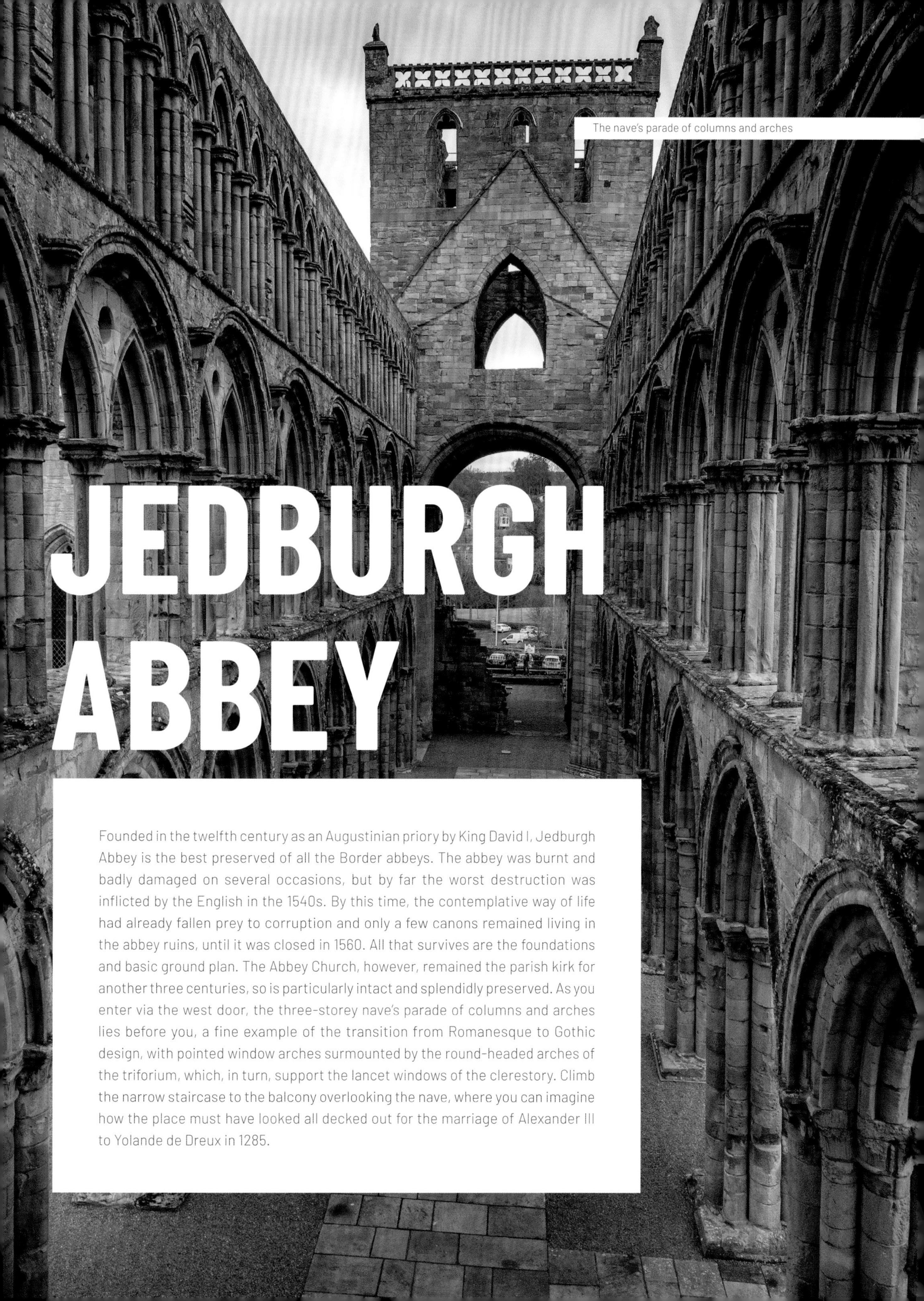

The nave's parade of columns and arches

JEDBURGH ABBEY

Founded in the twelfth century as an Augustinian priory by King David I, Jedburgh Abbey is the best preserved of all the Border abbeys. The abbey was burnt and badly damaged on several occasions, but by far the worst destruction was inflicted by the English in the 1540s. By this time, the contemplative way of life had already fallen prey to corruption and only a few canons remained living in the abbey ruins, until it was closed in 1560. All that survives are the foundations and basic ground plan. The Abbey Church, however, remained the parish kirk for another three centuries, so is particularly intact and splendidly preserved. As you enter via the west door, the three-storey nave's parade of columns and arches lies before you, a fine example of the transition from Romanesque to Gothic design, with pointed window arches surmounted by the round-headed arches of the triforium, which, in turn, support the lancet windows of the clerestory. Climb the narrow staircase to the balcony overlooking the nave, where you can imagine how the place must have looked all decked out for the marriage of Alexander III to Yolande de Dreux in 1285.

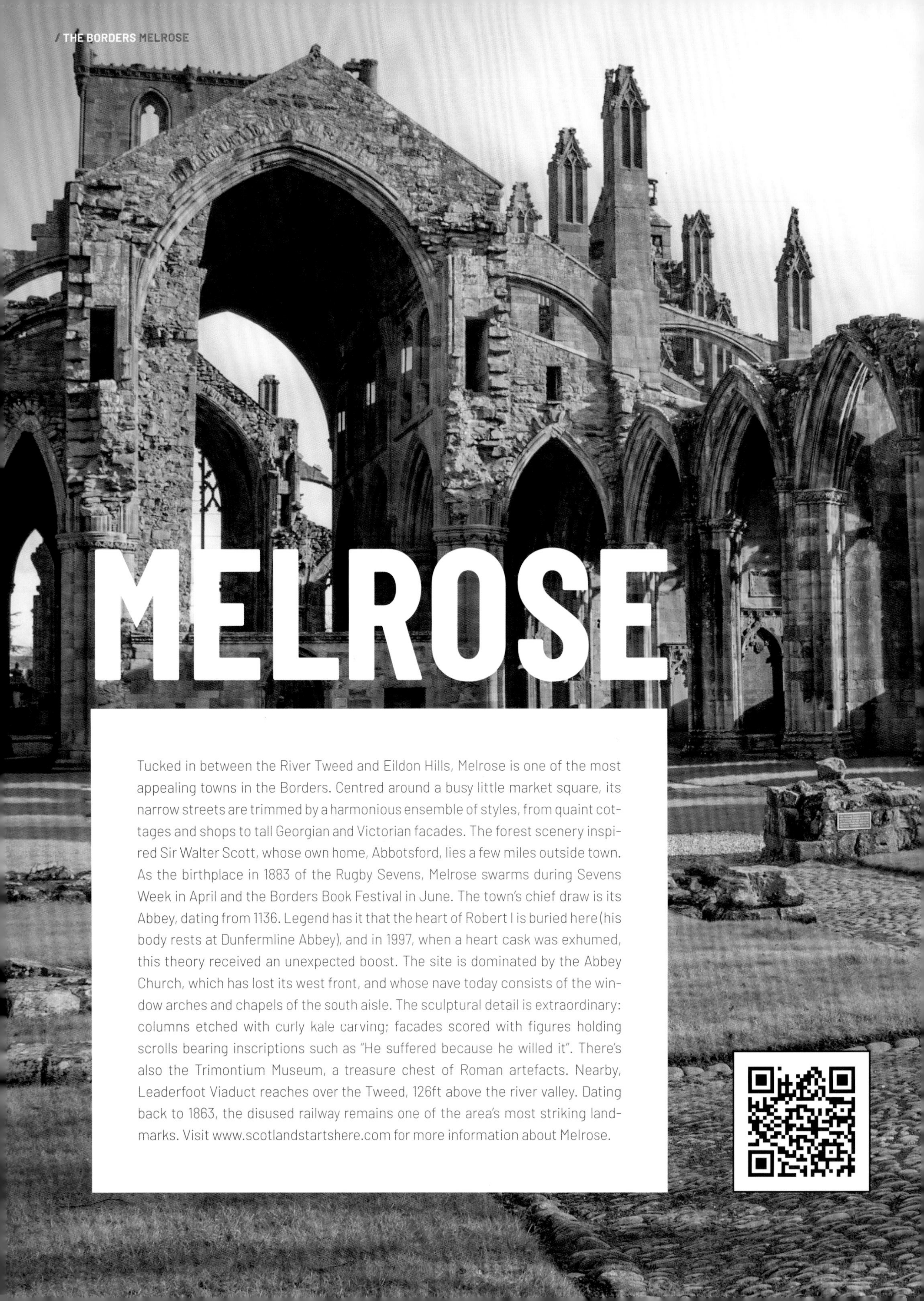

MELROSE

Tucked in between the River Tweed and Eildon Hills, Melrose is one of the most appealing towns in the Borders. Centred around a busy little market square, its narrow streets are trimmed by a harmonious ensemble of styles, from quaint cottages and shops to tall Georgian and Victorian facades. The forest scenery inspired Sir Walter Scott, whose own home, Abbotsford, lies a few miles outside town. As the birthplace in 1883 of the Rugby Sevens, Melrose swarms during Sevens Week in April and the Borders Book Festival in June. The town's chief draw is its Abbey, dating from 1136. Legend has it that the heart of Robert I is buried here (his body rests at Dunfermline Abbey), and in 1997, when a heart cask was exhumed, this theory received an unexpected boost. The site is dominated by the Abbey Church, which has lost its west front, and whose nave today consists of the window arches and chapels of the south aisle. The sculptural detail is extraordinary: columns etched with curly kale carving; facades scored with figures holding scrolls bearing inscriptions such as "He suffered because he willed it". There's also the Trimontium Museum, a treasure chest of Roman artefacts. Nearby, Leaderfoot Viaduct reaches over the Tweed, 126ft above the river valley. Dating back to 1863, the disused railway remains one of the area's most striking landmarks. Visit www.scotlandstartshere.com for more information about Melrose.

Abbotsford gardens

Sir Walter Scott's home, Abbotsford

Melrose is lined with characterful cafés

Borders Book Festival hits the town in June

Peebles Old Parish Church and the Tweed Bridge

The scenic Sware Trail passes Neidpath Castle

The surrounding countryside is a cycling hotspot

The High Street is bordered by a medley of architectural styles

Peebles unfurls from the banks of the River Tweed

PEEBLES

Fast, wide, tree-lined and fringed with grassy paths, the River Tweed looks its best at Peebles, a handsome royal burgh draped across the north bank, 22 miles south of the capital. The town has a genteel, relaxed air, its wide High Street bordered by houses in a medley of architectural styles, mostly dating from Victorian times. Plenty of enticing shops, restaurants and tearooms cater to day-trippers from Edinburgh. Nearby, a series of footpaths snakes through the rough-edged burns, bare peaks and deep wooded hills of the surrounding Peebles. The five-mile Sware Trail is one of the easiest and most scenic, weaving along the north bank of the river and looping back to the south. On the way, it passes Neidpath Castle, a gaunt medieval tower house perched high on a rocky bluff. Other, longer footpaths follow the old drove roads, like the thirteen-mile haul to St Mary's Loch or the fourteen-mile route to Selkirk via Traquair House. For a gentler stroll there's a three-mile amble downstream on the Tweed's banks to the privately owned Kailzie Gardens.

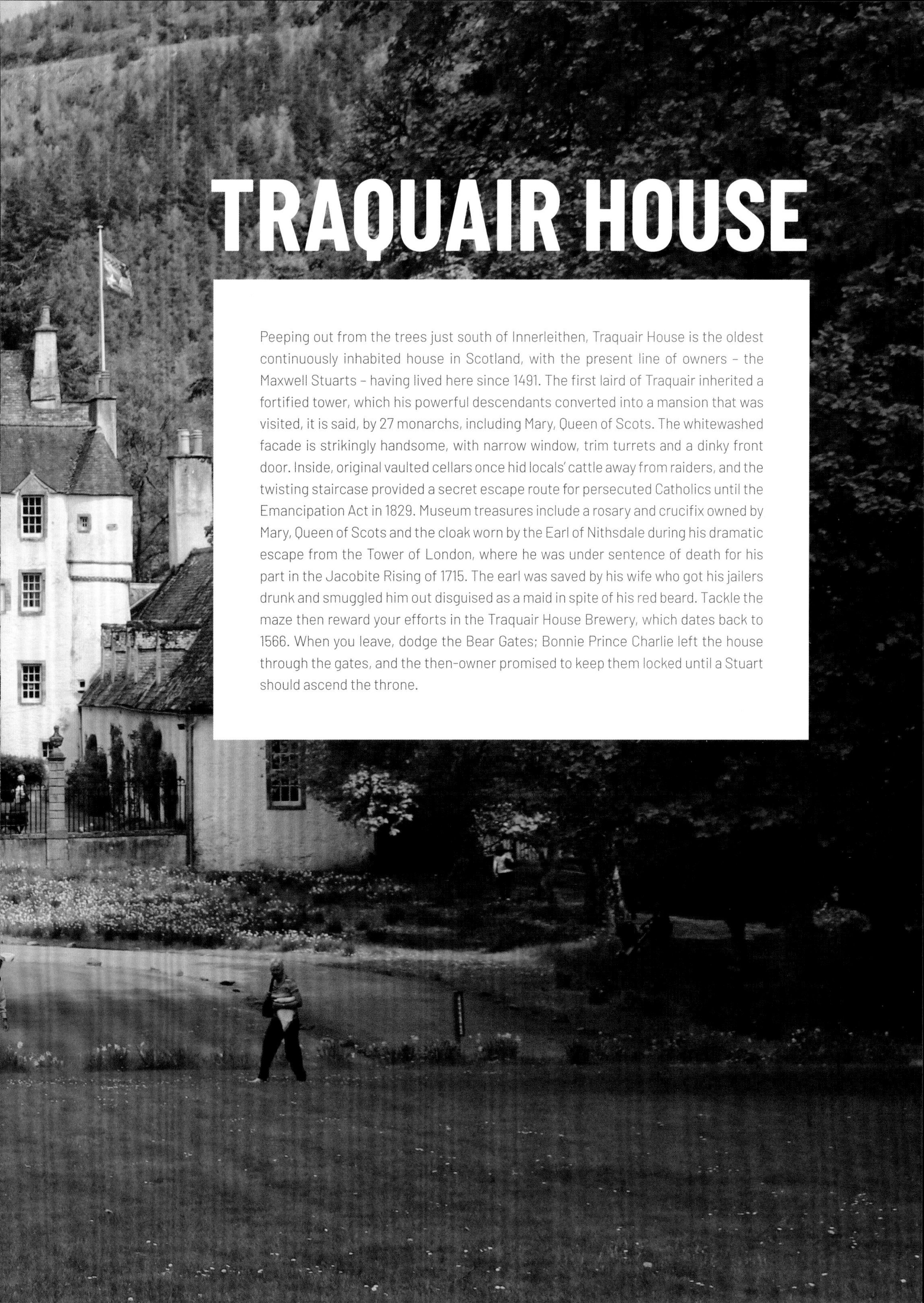

TRAQUAIR HOUSE

Peeping out from the trees just south of Innerleithen, Traquair House is the oldest continuously inhabited house in Scotland, with the present line of owners – the Maxwell Stuarts – having lived here since 1491. The first laird of Traquair inherited a fortified tower, which his powerful descendants converted into a mansion that was visited, it is said, by 27 monarchs, including Mary, Queen of Scots. The whitewashed facade is strikingly handsome, with narrow window, trim turrets and a dinky front door. Inside, original vaulted cellars once hid locals' cattle away from raiders, and the twisting staircase provided a secret escape route for persecuted Catholics until the Emancipation Act in 1829. Museum treasures include a rosary and crucifix owned by Mary, Queen of Scots and the cloak worn by the Earl of Nithsdale during his dramatic escape from the Tower of London, where he was under sentence of death for his part in the Jacobite Rising of 1715. The earl was saved by his wife who got his jailers drunk and smuggled him out disguised as a maid in spite of his red beard. Tackle the maze then reward your efforts in the Traquair House Brewery, which dates back to 1566. When you leave, dodge the Bear Gates; Bonnie Prince Charlie left the house through the gates, and the then-owner promised to keep them locked until a Stuart should ascend the throne.

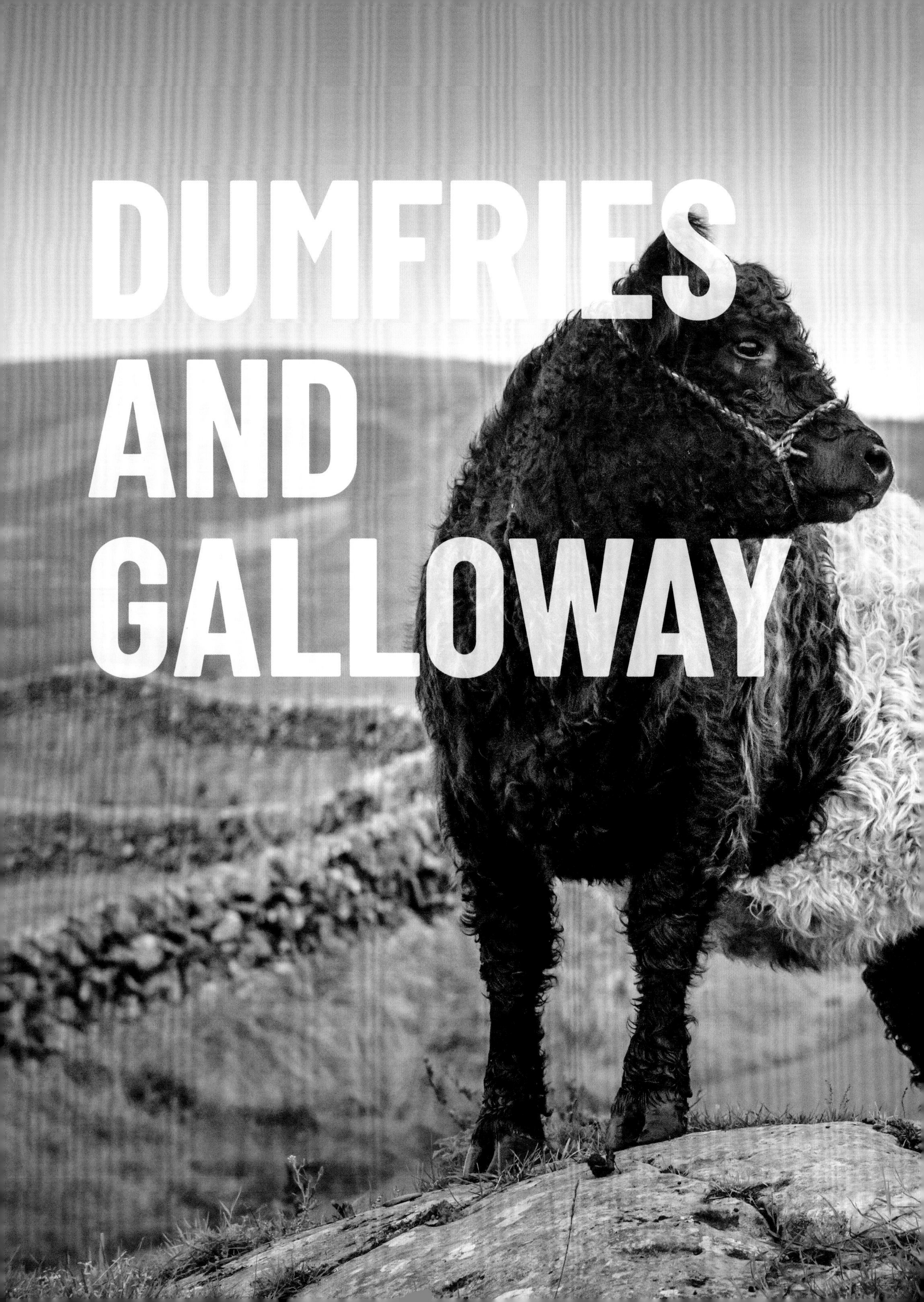
DUMFRIES
AND
GALLOWAY

The ornate Renaissance facade of the Nithsdale Lodging

Looking up one of the turrets

One of the few triangular fortresses in the world

The old stones are etched with history

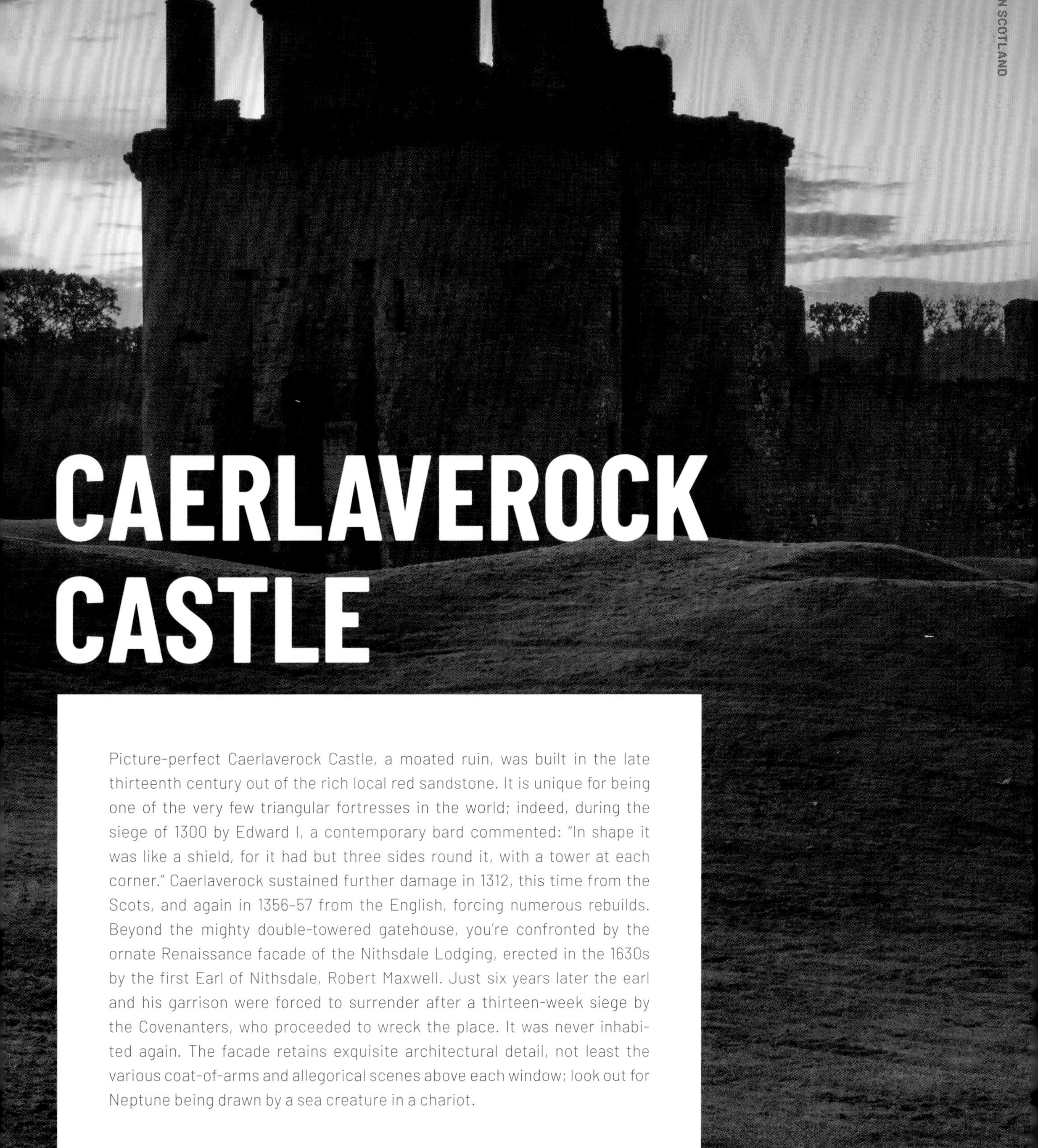

CAERLAVEROCK CASTLE

Picture-perfect Caerlaverock Castle, a moated ruin, was built in the late thirteenth century out of the rich local red sandstone. It is unique for being one of the very few triangular fortresses in the world; indeed, during the siege of 1300 by Edward I, a contemporary bard commented: "In shape it was like a shield, for it had but three sides round it, with a tower at each corner." Caerlaverock sustained further damage in 1312, this time from the Scots, and again in 1356–57 from the English, forcing numerous rebuilds. Beyond the mighty double-towered gatehouse, you're confronted by the ornate Renaissance facade of the Nithsdale Lodging, erected in the 1630s by the first Earl of Nithsdale, Robert Maxwell. Just six years later the earl and his garrison were forced to surrender after a thirteen-week siege by the Covenanters, who proceeded to wreck the place. It was never inhabited again. The facade retains exquisite architectural detail, not least the various coat-of-arms and allegorical scenes above each window; look out for Neptune being drawn by a sea creature in a chariot.

GALLOWAY FOREST PARK

Britain's largest forest and first Dark Sky Park, Galloway Forest Park stretches 774 square kilometres across the Galloway glens and hills. The park has three visitor centres with graded walking trails that crisscross the peaceful woodland; Kirroughtree and Glentrool also have excellent mountain-biking facilities with trailheads and bike hire. The third, Clatteringshaws has a lovely lochside café and is an easy stroll to the granite stone where Robert the Bruce is said to have rested after victory against the English in 1307. From here, follow the Gariland Burn to Loch Neldricken and Loch Enoch, with their silver granite sands, and then on to the Devil's Bowling Green, strewn with hundreds of erratic boulders left by the retreating glaciers. Potential wildlife sightings in the park include red squirrels, red deer (there's a hide at the Red Deer Range if the creatures prove elusive) and the back-from-near-extinction red kite. The Raiders' Road, a 16km route tracing the River Dee, is a scenic drive dotted with waterfalls and natural pools where you can swim. Thanks to a lack of light pollution, the park offers out--of-this-world stargazing; the finest locations include the visitor centres, Loch Trool, Loch Braden and Loch Doon Castle.

The Southern Upland Way skirts Loch Trool

Hides at Red Deer Range offer excellent wildlife-watching

Mist-shrouded vistas from the Glen of the Bar viewpoint

Britain's first Dark Sky Park is perfect for stargazing

Thirty acres of sculpture gardens to explore

Charles Jencks' trademark sculpted mounds

Black Hole Terrace

Artworks play with space and illusion

THE GARDEN OF COSMIC SPECULATION

There aren't many gardens that could live up to such a grandiloquent title but Charles Jencks' masterpiece fits the bill. The fact that public access is limited to one day a year only adds to the allure. Across thirty acres of Dumfriesshire countryside, the late doyen of landscape design translated his "cosmic" goal of finding relationships between the big and small, science and spirituality, the universe and the landscape. Trademark contoured mounds echo prehistoric barrows, Incan terraces and the Nazca Lines, while evoking the mindbending infinity of fractals. The Black Hole Terrace deepens the optical illusion, warping time and space with its chequerboard of Astroturf and metal sheeting, accompanied by a metallic double helix. Elsewhere, sculpted and bisected pools recall both the earth's oceanic beginnings and the causeways of ancient Mexico.

Echoes of prehistoric barrows, Incan terraces and the Nazca Lines

KIRKCUDBRIGHT

A handsome little harbour town of broad streets and brightly painted houses, Kirkcudbright ("kir-coo-bree") has long been a favoured haunt for artists and painters, none more so than the revered "Glasgow Boys", who sought inspiration in its unique combination of light and landscape. One such artist was Edward Hornel (an associate of the Glasgow Boys), whose life and work you can admire at Broughton House where he resided between 1901 and his death in 1933; these days, his old studio is given over to an artist in residence. For an overview of these chaps, as well as some of Scotland's other famous artists, pop into the shiny Kirkcudbright Galleries. The town also rates a clutch of other eminently appealing sites, from the sturdy MacLellan's Castle to one of the most haphazardly enjoyable collections you'll find anywhere, courtesy of the Stewartry Museum, which holds objects as diverse as clay pipes and pickled fish.

RHINS OF GALLOWAY

For a real sense of perspective, few trips in Scotland beat the contemplative quiet of the Rhins of Galloway. The country's southernmost point, the hammer-headed peninsula is visible from afar and along the coast thanks to the chess piece-style Mull of Galloway Lighthouse. The sense of remoteness is palpable, whether you're taking a cliff walk to the foghorn and viewing platform overlooking the 260ft-high cliffs, or visiting the RSPB visitor centre to loop through the bird-nested heathland. Climb the 115 steps to the top of the lighthouse for epic vistas, or go for a bracing dip on one of the sandy beaches lacing the peninsula. Some of the finest strands are the coves beside the harbour town of Portpatrick and those wrapping around Victorian-era Knockinaam Lodge, where Sir Winston Churchill plotted D-Day from his favourite hotel room. Check out the Mull of Galloway Experience (March–Oct) at www.mull-of-galloway.co.uk, or visit www.scotlandstartshere.com for more information on Galloway.

The sandy beach at Portpatrick

Mull of Galloway Lighthouse

The hammer-headed peninsula anchors southwest Scotland

The Open Book

Wigtown: Scotland's answer to Hay-on-Wye

Vintage tomes in The Book Shop

The Book Shop: does what it says on the tin

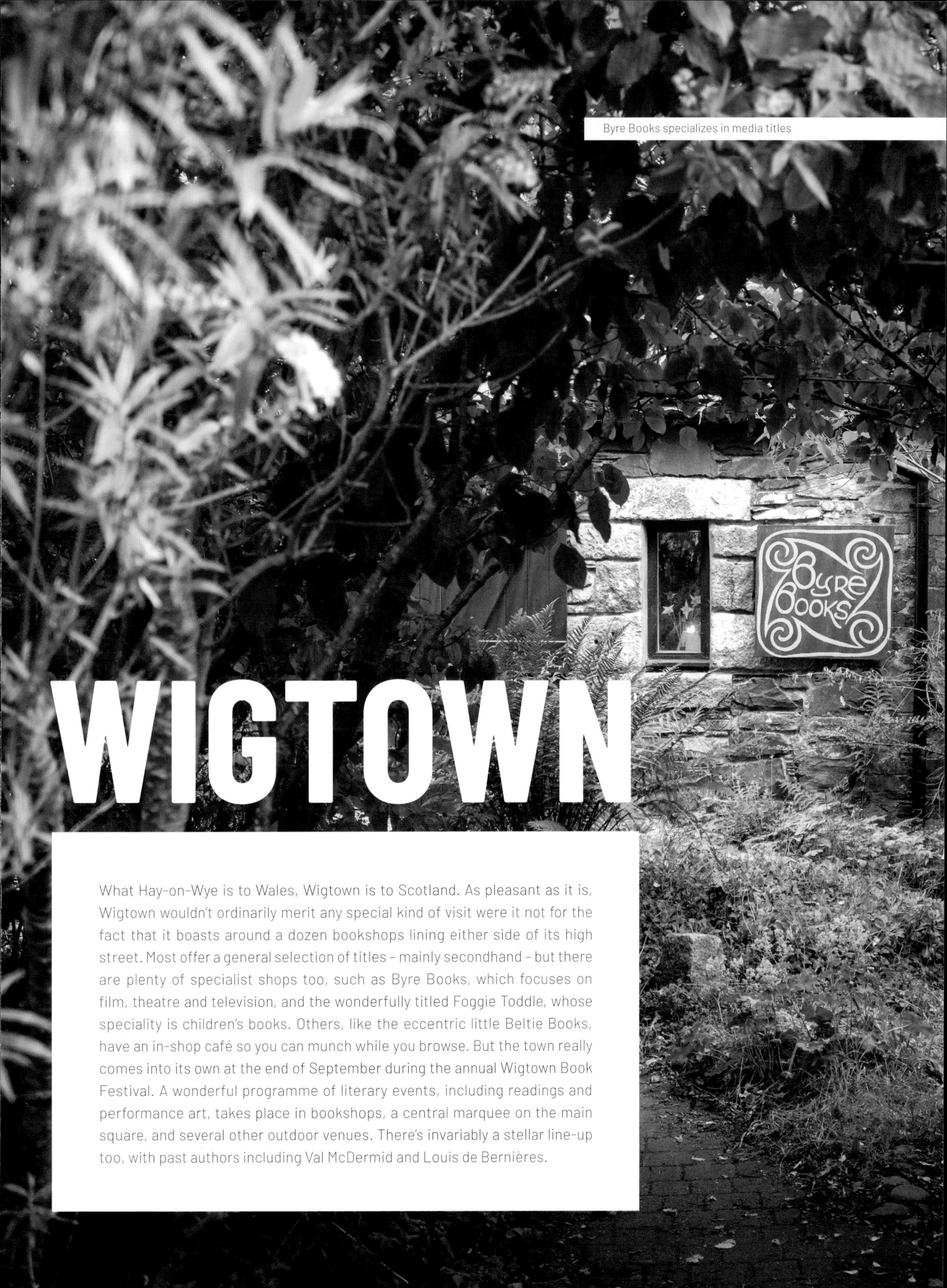

Byre Books specializes in media titles

WIGTOWN

What Hay-on-Wye is to Wales, Wigtown is to Scotland. As pleasant as it is, Wigtown wouldn't ordinarily merit any special kind of visit were it not for the fact that it boasts around a dozen bookshops lining either side of its high street. Most offer a general selection of titles – mainly secondhand – but there are plenty of specialist shops too, such as Byre Books, which focuses on film, theatre and television, and the wonderfully titled Foggie Toddle, whose speciality is children's books. Others, like the eccentric little Beltie Books, have an in-shop café so you can munch while you browse. But the town really comes into its own at the end of September during the annual Wigtown Book Festival. A wonderful programme of literary events, including readings and performance art, takes place in bookshops, a central marquee on the main square, and several other outdoor venues. There's invariably a stellar line-up too, with past authors including Val McDermid and Louis de Bernières.

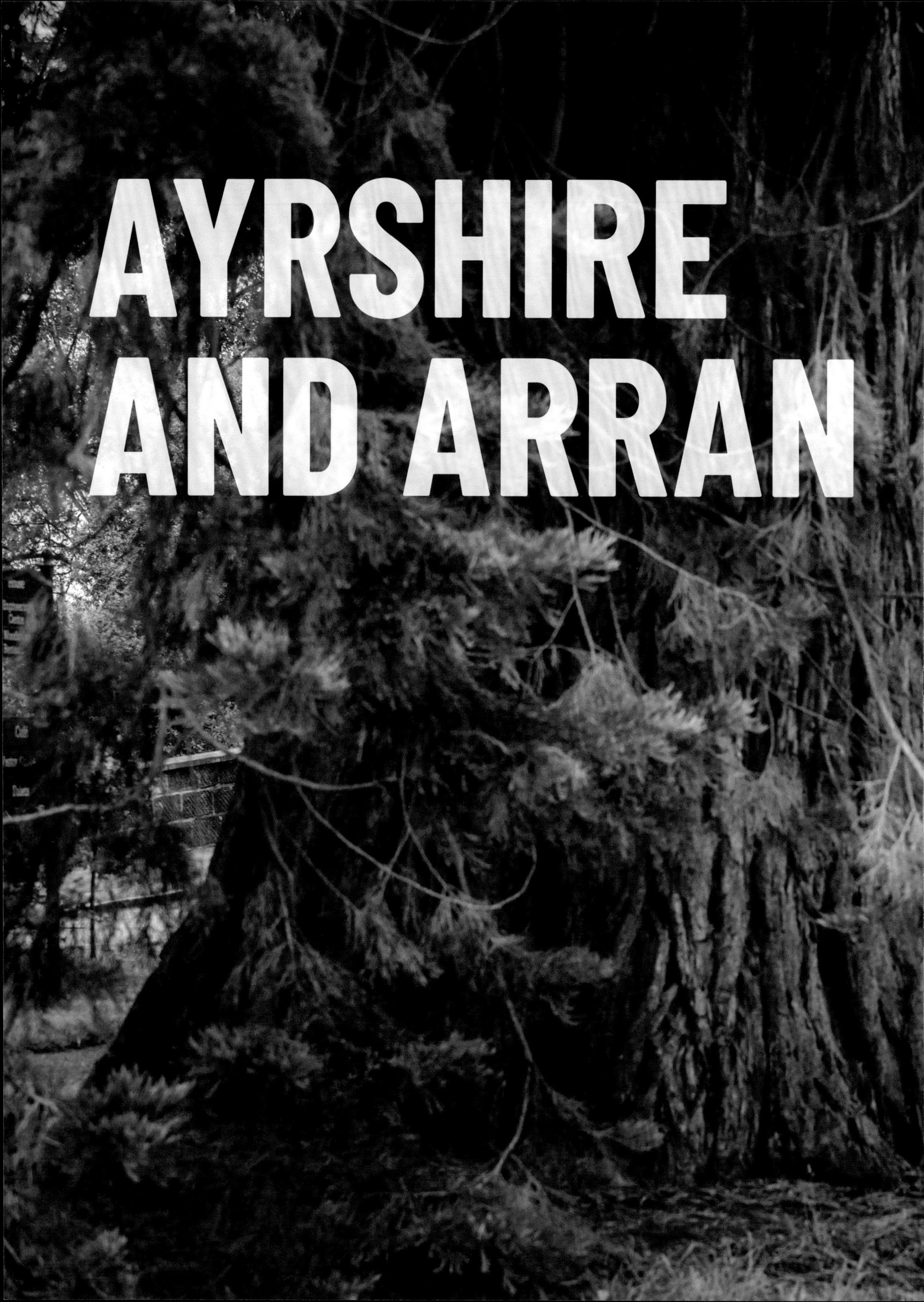

AYRSHIRE AND ARRAN

AILSA CRAIG

As you travel along the South Ayrshire coast, the giant muffin-shaped island of Ailsa Craig is an intriguing presence on the horizon, stranded as it is in the middle of the Firth of Clyde. The island's name means "Fairy Rock" in Gaelic, though it was a less than enchanting place for the persecuted Catholics who escaped here during the Reformation. The island's granite has long been used for making what many consider to be the finest curling stones – a company in nearby Mauchline still has exclusive rights and sporadically collects a few boulders. In the late nineteenth century, 29 people lived on the island, either working in the quarry or at the Stevenson lighthouse. With its volcanic, columnar cliffs and 1114ft summit, Ailsa Craig is now a bird sanctuary that's home to some 40,000 gannets, plus thousands of other seabirds. Visit at the end of May and in June to see the fledglings trying to fly. Trips to the island depart from Girvan, 21 miles south of Ayr. It takes about an hour to reach the island, after which you get enough time to walk up to the summit of the rock and watch the birds, weather permitting.

A riot of colourful wildflowers in spring

Hiking on Goat Fell, north Arran's mountain range

North Glen Sannox

King's Cave, where Robert the Bruce rested before the Battle of Bannockburn

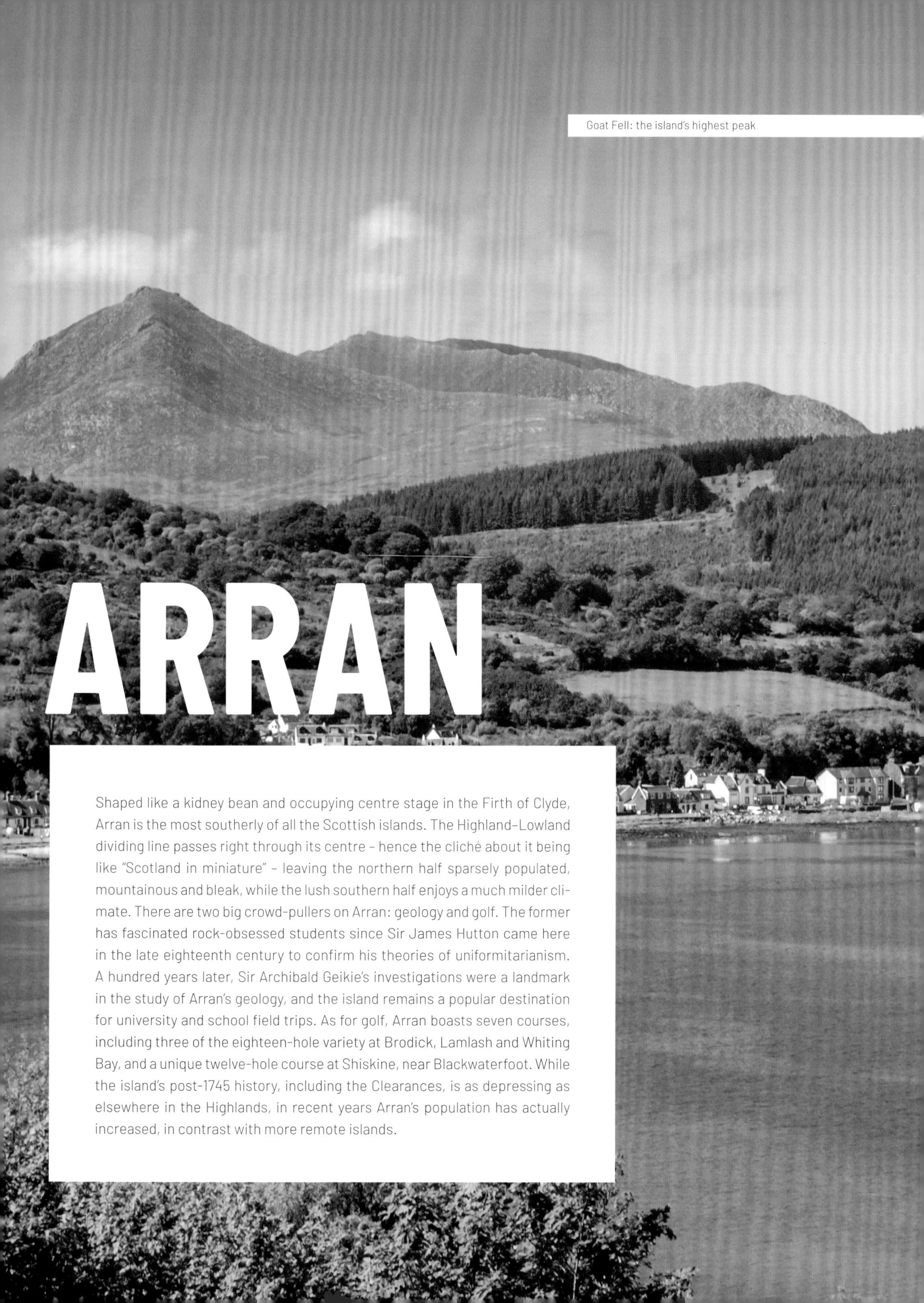

Goat Fell: the island's highest peak

ARRAN

Shaped like a kidney bean and occupying centre stage in the Firth of Clyde, Arran is the most southerly of all the Scottish islands. The Highland–Lowland dividing line passes right through its centre – hence the cliché about it being like "Scotland in miniature" – leaving the northern half sparsely populated, mountainous and bleak, while the lush southern half enjoys a much milder climate. There are two big crowd-pullers on Arran: geology and golf. The former has fascinated rock-obsessed students since Sir James Hutton came here in the late eighteenth century to confirm his theories of uniformitarianism. A hundred years later, Sir Archibald Geikie's investigations were a landmark in the study of Arran's geology, and the island remains a popular destination for university and school field trips. As for golf, Arran boasts seven courses, including three of the eighteen-hole variety at Brodick, Lamlash and Whiting Bay, and a unique twelve-hole course at Shiskine, near Blackwaterfoot. While the island's post-1745 history, including the Clearances, is as depressing as elsewhere in the Highlands, in recent years Arran's population has actually increased, in contrast with more remote islands.

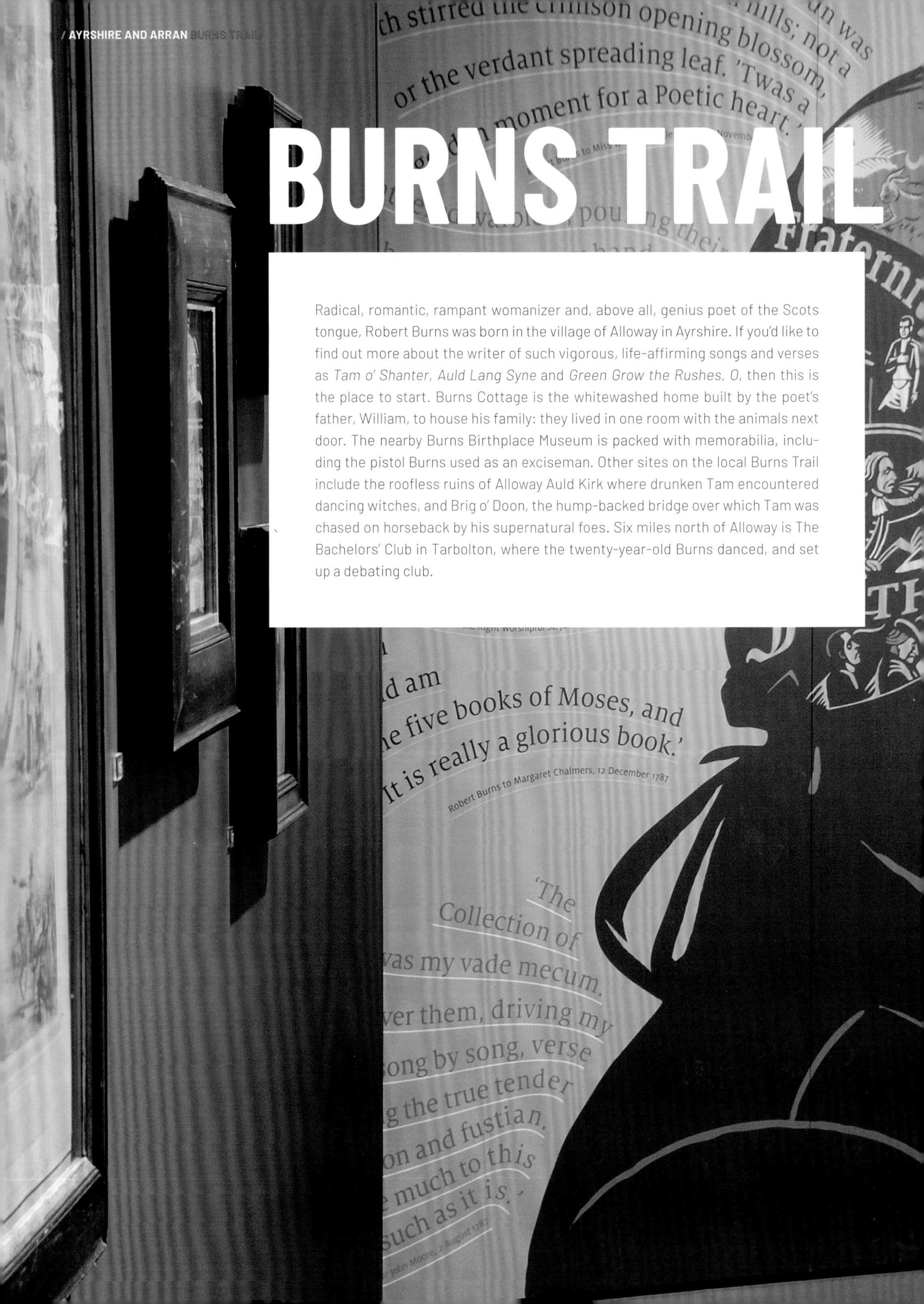

BURNS TRAIL

Radical, romantic, rampant womanizer and, above all, genius poet of the Scots tongue, Robert Burns was born in the village of Alloway in Ayrshire. If you'd like to find out more about the writer of such vigorous, life-affirming songs and verses as *Tam o' Shanter*, *Auld Lang Syne* and *Green Grow the Rushes, O*, then this is the place to start. Burns Cottage is the whitewashed home built by the poet's father, William, to house his family: they lived in one room with the animals next door. The nearby Burns Birthplace Museum is packed with memorabilia, including the pistol Burns used as an exciseman. Other sites on the local Burns Trail include the roofless ruins of Alloway Auld Kirk where drunken Tam encountered dancing witches, and Brig o' Doon, the hump-backed bridge over which Tam was chased on horseback by his supernatural foes. Six miles north of Alloway is The Bachelors' Club in Tarbolton, where the twenty-year-old Burns danced, and set up a debating club.

Burns Cottage, built by the poet's father

Alloway Auld Kirk

Brig o' Doon

Culzean Castle from Croy Beach

Fountain-dotted gardens

Fans of the castle include former US President Eisenhower

Deer park

Seven ghosts are rumoured to haunt the corridors

CULZEAN CASTLE

In a country that has more than its fair share of heart-pounding castles, it takes something special to take your breath away. Though it is conceived with the same baronial grace as so many in the Highlands, Culzean Castle steals the show thanks to its awe-inspiring location. From its cliff-hugging perch above sculpted coves that recast the sun-drowsy Ayrshire coast as the Adriatic, the turreted 16th-century abode appears as though it was built on top of the crashing Atlantic waves. Guides will tell you that the castle made a lasting impression on former US President Eisenhower when he stayed here while in office, but more fantastic are the rumours that seven ghosts haunt the corridors. Instead of spectres and ghouls, just hope you only find creaky stairways and stories of the lords and ladies who once lived here. The grounds are filled with twisted woods, secret follies, a walled garden, an ice house, clock tower, deer park and swan pond; a riot of colour in summer.

Dumfries House was commissioned by the fifth Earl of Dumfries

The house has an outstanding collection of Chippendale furniture

Chinese pagoda in the gardens

Chippendale grandfather clock

DUMFRIES HOUSE

A handsome Palladian villa, Dumfries House was commissioned by the fifth Earl of Dumfries, a widower who wanted to remarry and ensure that he had an heir for the family estate. The house, the first major early commission for the Adam brothers, was conceived as a honey trap to lure a potential wife, and, judging by the portrait of the ageing, gouty earl in the Pink Drawing Room, he needed all the help he could get. Such was the earl's urgency, the house was built and decked out swiftly – between 1756 and 1760 – meaning its Rococo decor is in perfect harmony with the graceful sandstone exterior. The earl secured a wife but died without producing an heir; the family subsequently turned their attention to creating Mount Stuart, leaving Dumfries House to be looked after by a series of housekeepers. The recent story of the house is as remarkable as its past: the building and its contents were all up for sale in 2007, and some of the furniture had begun its journey south to Christie's when Prince Charles and a hastily assembled trust intervened to make a heritage "save". Chief among the treasures is an outstanding collection of Chippendale furniture, including a truly spectacular, one-of-a-kind rosewood bookcase, reputedly now worth around £20 million.

GLASGOW AND THE CLYDE

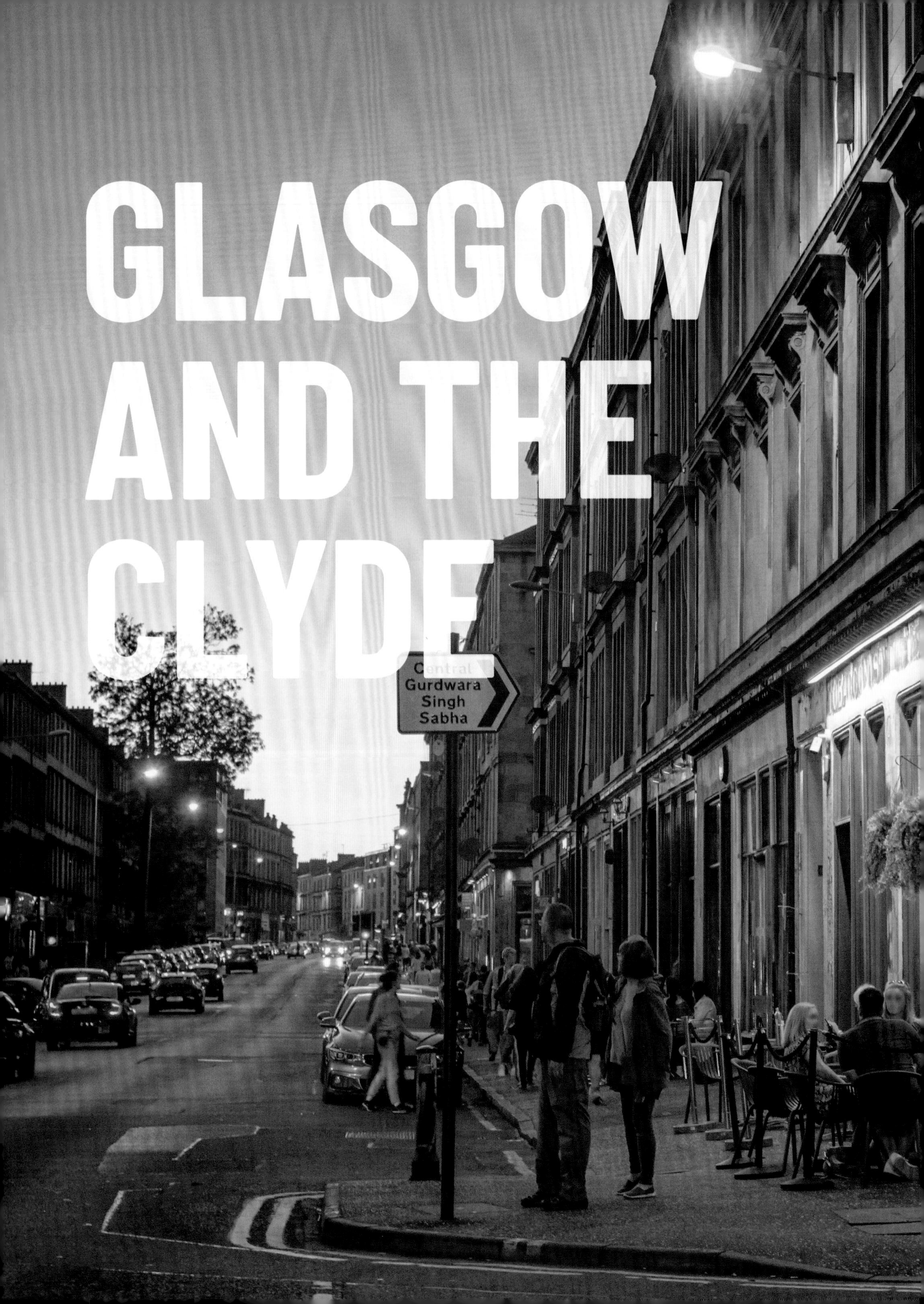

The CRESCENT
Restricted parking ZONE
Park only in signed bays
CRESCENT
SERVED ALL DAY

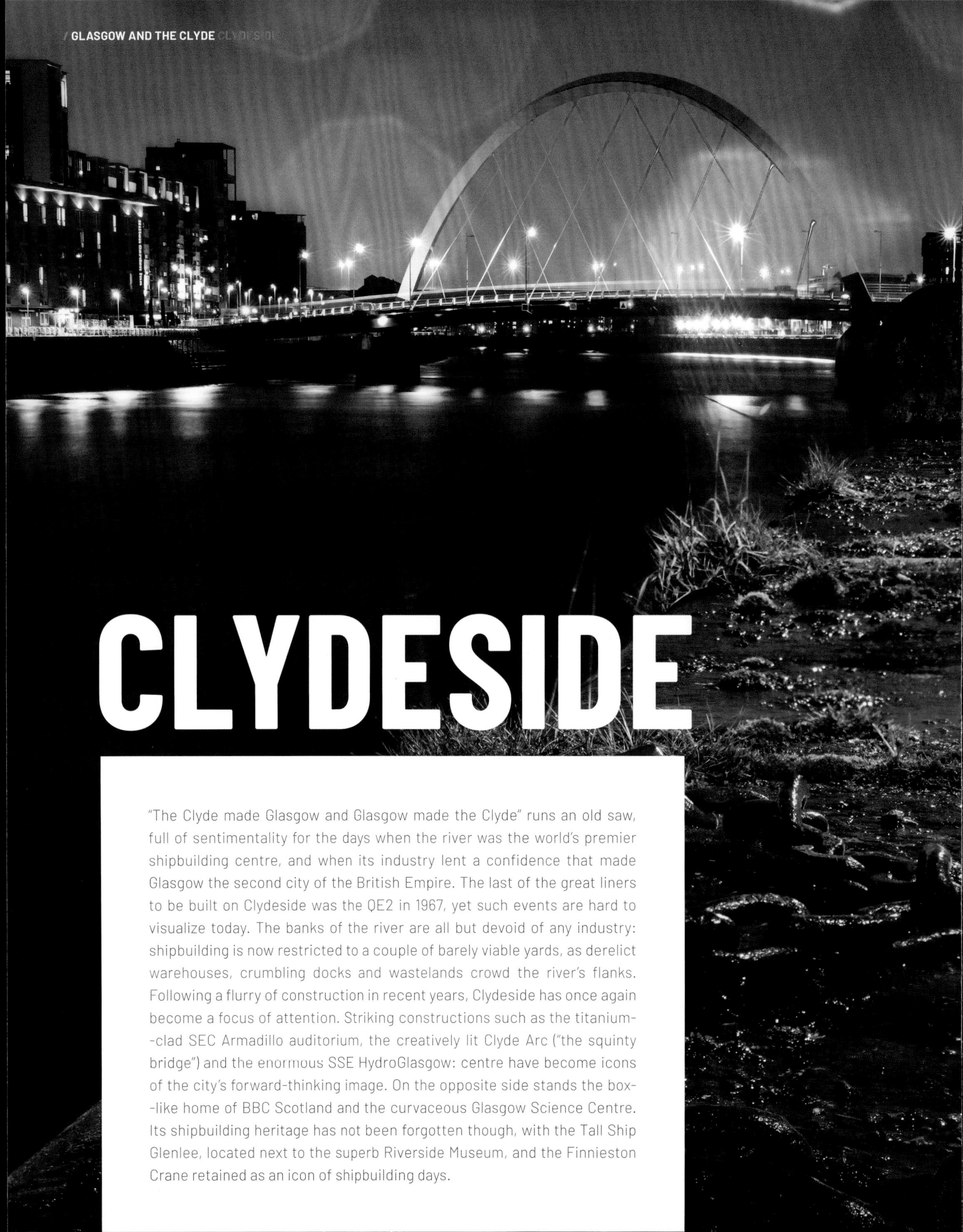

CLYDESIDE

"The Clyde made Glasgow and Glasgow made the Clyde" runs an old saw, full of sentimentality for the days when the river was the world's premier shipbuilding centre, and when its industry lent a confidence that made Glasgow the second city of the British Empire. The last of the great liners to be built on Clydeside was the QE2 in 1967, yet such events are hard to visualize today. The banks of the river are all but devoid of any industry: shipbuilding is now restricted to a couple of barely viable yards, as derelict warehouses, crumbling docks and wastelands crowd the river's flanks. Following a flurry of construction in recent years, Clydeside has once again become a focus of attention. Striking constructions such as the titanium--clad SEC Armadillo auditorium, the creatively lit Clyde Arc ("the squinty bridge") and the enormous SSE HydroGlasgow: centre have become icons of the city's forward-thinking image. On the opposite side stands the box--like home of BBC Scotland and the curvaceous Glasgow Science Centre. Its shipbuilding heritage has not been forgotten though, with the Tall Ship Glenlee, located next to the superb Riverside Museum, and the Finnieston Crane retained as an icon of shipbuilding days.

Riverside Museum

SEC Armadillo

Glasgow Tower and IMAX

Finnieston Crane

Laboratorio Espresso, at the fore of Glasgow's burgeoning coffee scene

A short but sweet coffee menu is on offer at Spitfire Espresso

Cakes at Laboratorio

Spitfire Espresso uses Gunnerbean coffee from Colombia and Brazil

LABORATORIO

Get your caffeine kicks in Glasgow with a double shot of espresso in one of the city's cool artisan coffee houses such as Laboratorio or The "Lab", as it's more popularly known. One of the trailblazers at the fore of Glasgow's burgeoning coffee scene, this terrific little bolthole is decked out with cement board walls and recycled wood panelling. Super-friendly baristas really do know their beans; there's typically a single-origin espresso and a guest espresso on the go at any one time. You can perch inside, takeaway or grab one of the sought-after pavement tables. Another fine addition to the city's roster of artisan coffee houses, Spitfire Espresso is a light and airy space, with turquoise painted window frames set against cream walls and a scattering of tables outside facing a large street art mural. There's a short but enticing coffee menu, using Gunnerbean coffee from Colombia and Brazil. For something a little punchier, Tinderbox is a split-level coffee house serving half a dozen varieties of strong espressos to wash down its excellent fresh sandwiches and cakes.

Laboratorio or The "Lab", as it's more popularly known

NECROPOLIS

Rising up behind the cathedral, the atmospheric Necropolis is a grassy mound covered in a fantastic assortment of crumbling and tumbling gravestones, ornate urns, gloomy catacombs and Neoclassical temples. Inspired by the Père Lachaise cemetery in Paris, this garden of death was established in 1832, and it quickly became a fitting spot for the great and the good of wealthy nineteenth-century Glasgow to indulge their vanity; some 50,000 burials have taken place since the first one, and there are 3,500 monuments. Various paths lead through the rows of eroding, neglected graves, and from the summit, next to the column topped with an indignant John Knox, there are superb views of the cathedral below and the city beyond.

The Necropolis, inspired by Père Lachaise cemetery in Paris

RENNIE MACKINTOSH PILGRIMAGE

The work of the architect Charles Rennie Mackintosh (1868–1928) has come to be synonymous with the image of Glasgow. Historians may disagree over whether his work was a forerunner of the modernist movement or merely the sunset of Victorianism, but he undoubtedly created buildings of great beauty, idiosyncratically fusing Scots Baronial with Gothic, Art Nouveau and modern design. Mackintosh's big break came in 1896, when he won the competition to design a home for the Glasgow School of Art, now sadly damaged by two fires. A number of smaller buildings created during his tenure with the architects Honeyman and Keppie, which began in 1889, document the development of his style. One of his earliest commissions was for a new building to house the Glasgow Herald: The Lighthouse, now home to the Mackintosh Interpretation Centre, an illuminating trawl through the great man's work. In the 1890s Glasgow went wild for tearooms, and Mackintosh planned the interiors for what is now the Mackintosh at the Willow. The building that arguably displays the design visionary at his most flamboyant, however, was one he never saw built, the House for an Art Lover, constructed in Bellahouston Park in 1996, 95 years after the plans were submitted to a German architectural competition.

House for an Art Lover

Exhibition at Mackintosh at the Willow

The Mackintosh's reconstructed dining room at the Hunterian Museum

One of Glasgow's finest tearooms, Mackintosh at the Willow

Wester Ross

St Ninian's Cave

Roman Antonine Wall

Edinburgh Old Town

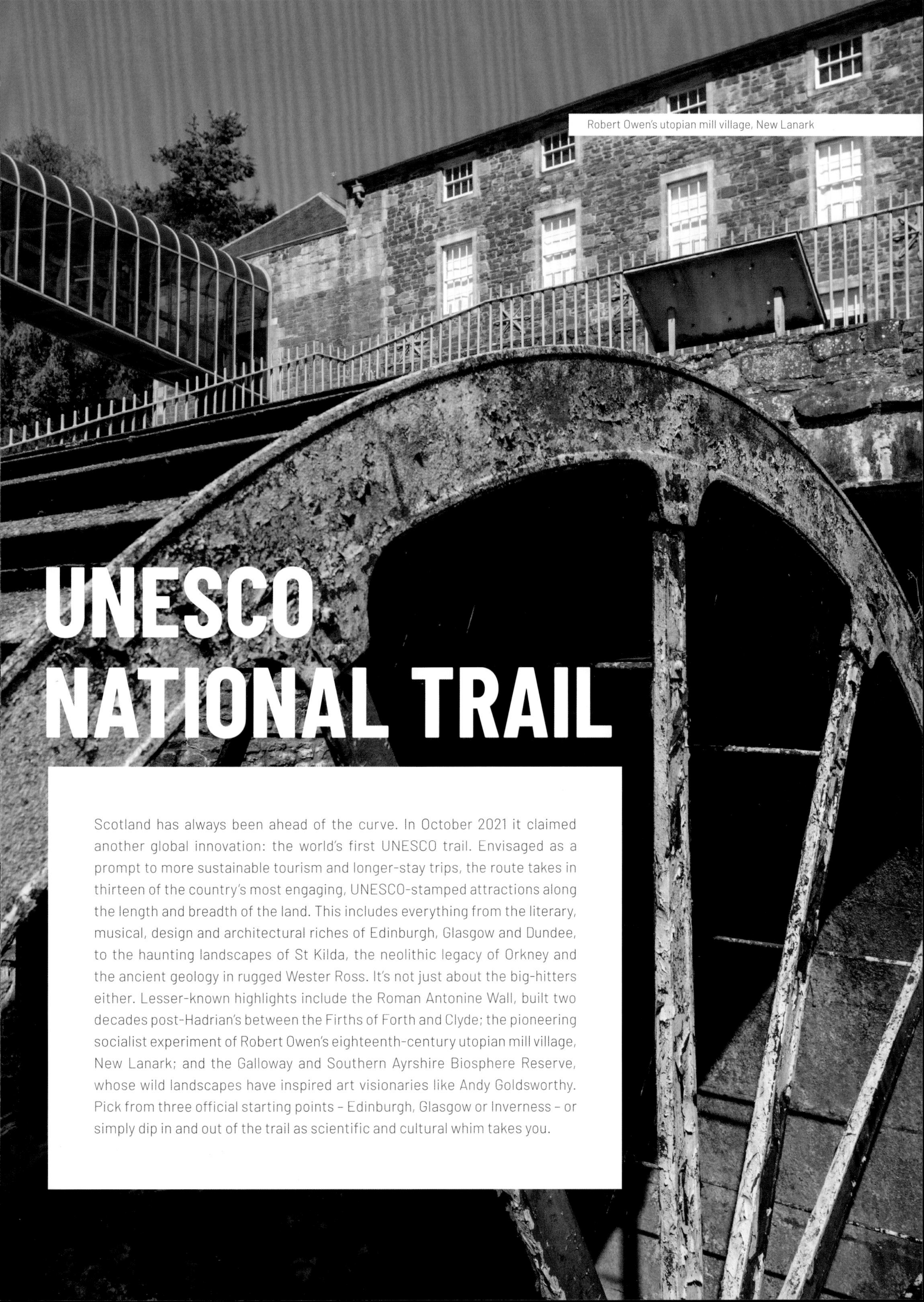

Robert Owen's utopian mill village, New Lanark

UNESCO NATIONAL TRAIL

Scotland has always been ahead of the curve. In October 2021 it claimed another global innovation: the world's first UNESCO trail. Envisaged as a prompt to more sustainable tourism and longer-stay trips, the route takes in thirteen of the country's most engaging, UNESCO-stamped attractions along the length and breadth of the land. This includes everything from the literary, musical, design and architectural riches of Edinburgh, Glasgow and Dundee, to the haunting landscapes of St Kilda, the neolithic legacy of Orkney and the ancient geology in rugged Wester Ross. It's not just about the big-hitters either. Lesser-known highlights include the Roman Antonine Wall, built two decades post-Hadrian's between the Firths of Forth and Clyde; the pioneering socialist experiment of Robert Owen's eighteenth-century utopian mill village, New Lanark; and the Galloway and Southern Ayrshire Biosphere Reserve, whose wild landscapes have inspired art visionaries like Andy Goldsworthy. Pick from three official starting points – Edinburgh, Glasgow or Inverness – or simply dip in and out of the trail as scientific and cultural whim takes you.

Glasgow's West End

Ashton Lane, a cobbled passageway off Byres Road

The grand tenements of the West End

Floating Heads Installation by Sophie Cave at Kelvingrove Art Gallery and Museum

Kelvingrove Art Gallery and Museum

WEST END

Glasgow's glamorous West End is a world away from the grim industrial image many people falsely hold of the city. In the 1800s the city's wealthy merchants set up their grand homes here, and in 1870 the ancient university was moved from its cramped home near the cathedral to a spacious new site overlooking the River Kelvin. Cultural riches await in the magnificent Kelvingrove Art Gallery and Museum, filled with works by Dalí, Rembrandt and Van Gogh, and the university's Hunterian Art Gallery, with its fine collection of paintings by James Abbott McNeill Whistler. Rolling Kelvingrove Park and the pleasure palace glass domes of the Botanic Gardens are the green lungs of the district. Bisecting the neighbourhood, Byres Road is a lively student hub, packed with bars, music venues and cafés.

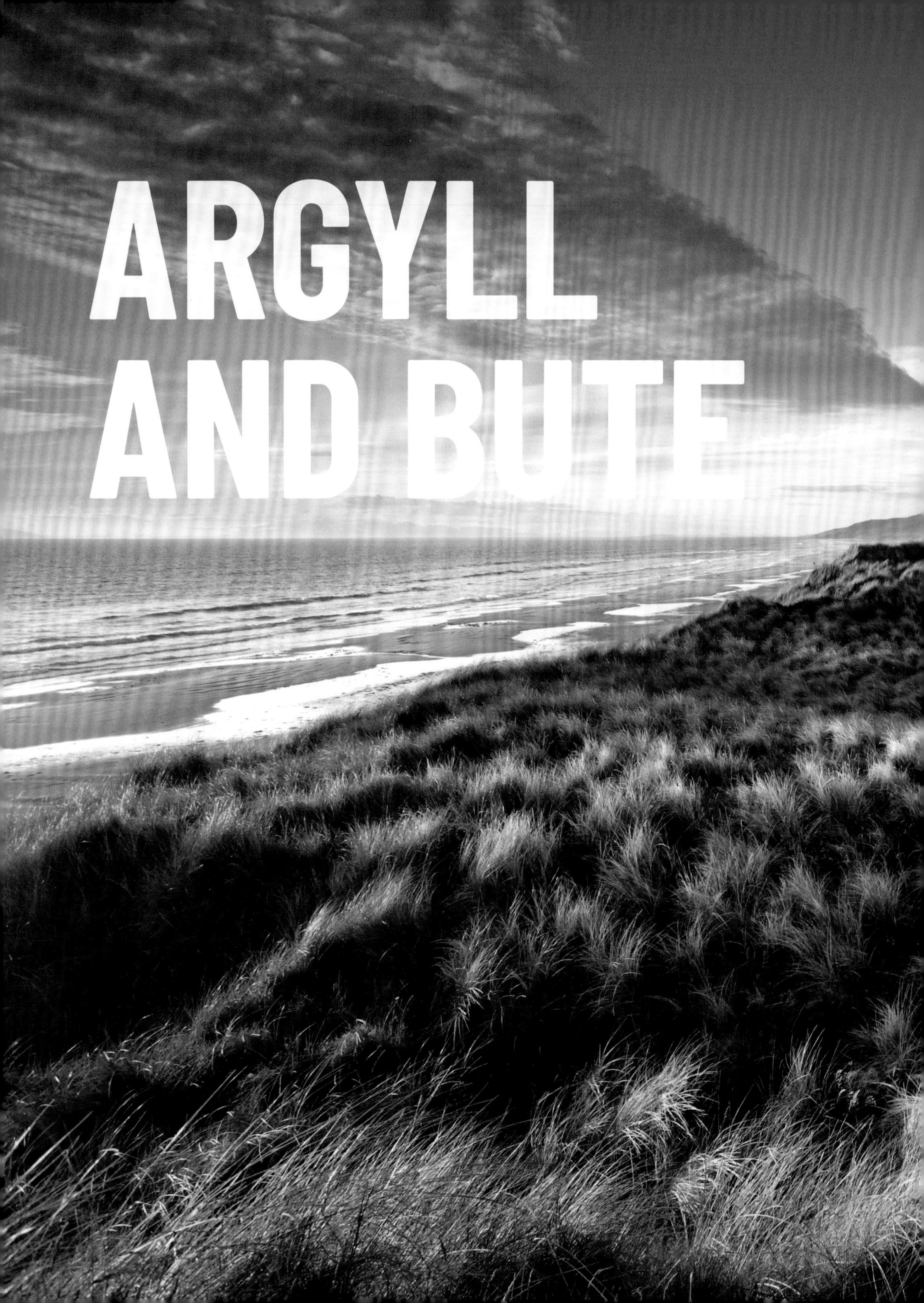

ARGYLL AND BUTE

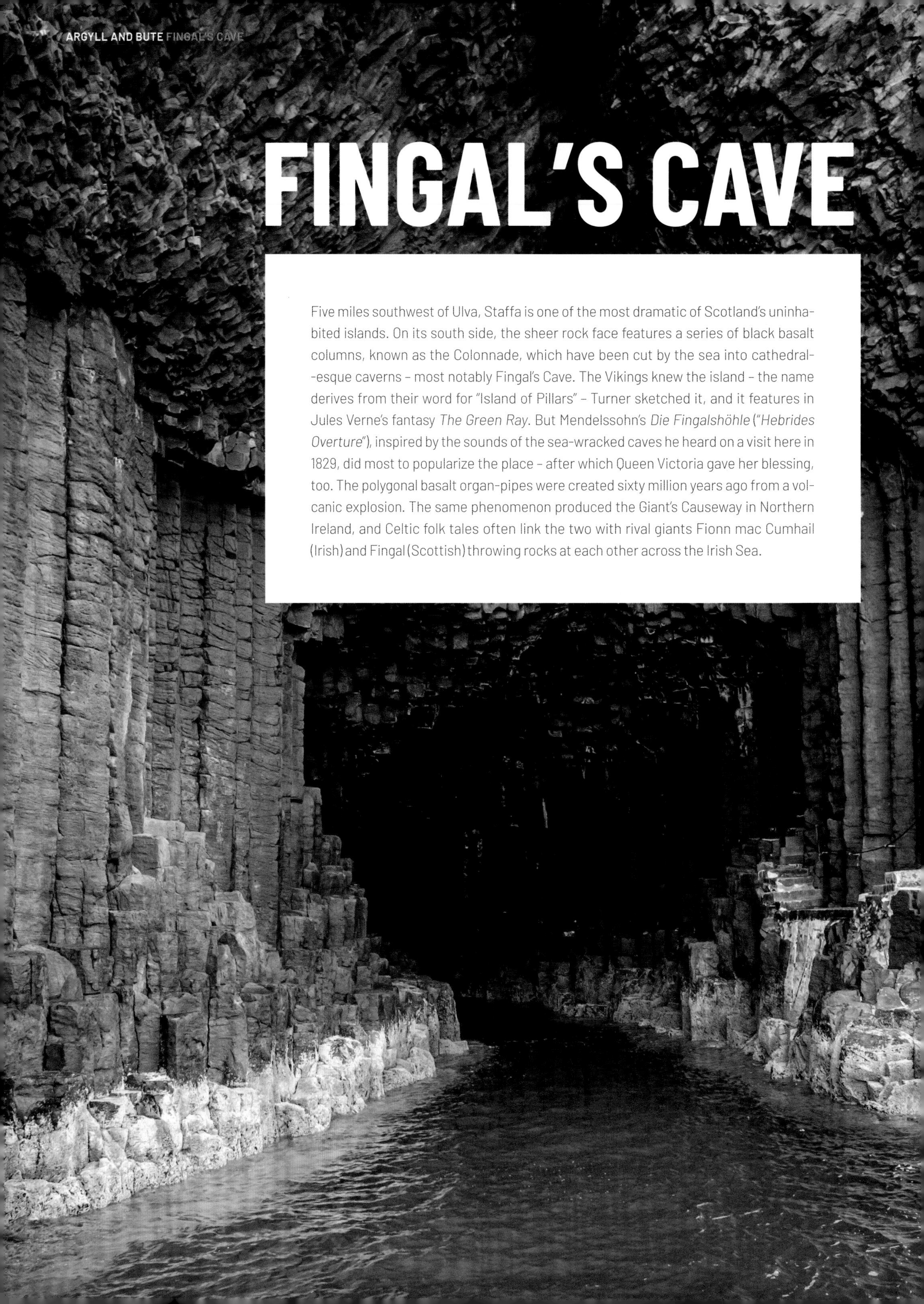

FINGAL'S CAVE

Five miles southwest of Ulva, Staffa is one of the most dramatic of Scotland's uninhabited islands. On its south side, the sheer rock face features a series of black basalt columns, known as the Colonnade, which have been cut by the sea into cathedral-esque caverns – most notably Fingal's Cave. The Vikings knew the island – the name derives from their word for "Island of Pillars" – Turner sketched it, and it features in Jules Verne's fantasy *The Green Ray*. But Mendelssohn's *Die Fingalshöhle* ("*Hebrides Overture*"), inspired by the sounds of the sea-wracked caves he heard on a visit here in 1829, did most to popularize the place – after which Queen Victoria gave her blessing, too. The polygonal basalt organ-pipes were created sixty million years ago from a volcanic explosion. The same phenomenon produced the Giant's Causeway in Northern Ireland, and Celtic folk tales often link the two with rival giants Fionn mac Cumhail (Irish) and Fingal (Scottish) throwing rocks at each other across the Irish Sea.

Staffa: one of the most dramatic of Scotland's uninhabited islands

Stone steps leading to Staffa's rugged coastline

Tourist boats call at Staffa

Exotic plants in Achamore Gardens

Freshly caught crab at the Boathouse Restaurant

Boathouse Restaurant on Ardminish Bay

Achamore Gardens, a 54-acre botanical wonderland

GIGHA

Rarely visited and ramshackle, yet all the better for it, this pint-sized speck is one of three outlying islands in the Southern Hebrides that tempt you out into the Atlantic. Like many of the smaller Hebrides, Gigha was bought and sold multiple times after its original lairds, the MacNeils, sold up, and was finally bought by the islanders themselves in 2002. Just six miles by one mile, Gigha has an almost tropical, Gulf Stream location, with tombola beaches, Caribbean-quality palms and the implausibly lovely Boathouse Restaurant serving local halibut and oysters right on the sand. There is just one hotel, one campsite and one ferry – but this is its safety net and shield. Those who do visit might need to plan ahead, but the rewards are plentiful. Kayak to footprint-free beaches, hike off-road trails with views of Islay, Jura and the distant blur of Ireland, and meander through Achamore Gardens, a 54-acre botanical wonderland brimming with rhododendrons, azaleas and New Zealand tree ferns. The ferry connects Kintyre on the mainland with the island, via a 20-minute boat ride.

Only one ferry carts passengers to Gigha

HEBRIDEAN WHALE TRAIL

There are plenty of land-based attractions among the pretty painted houses of Tobermory on the Isle of Mull – but wildlife opportunities galore await on the water. The boat trips off the west coast of Scotland are superb, offering visitors the chance to go in search of minke whales and orcas. Options include a seven-hour trip (not for under-12s) and a shorter four-hour version, plus a family-friendly 90-minute excursion to a seal colony. The experience itself is thrilling: imagine bouncing through the waves, binoculars at the ready, as an expert crew keep a watchful eye out for dolphins, porpoises, basking sharks and sea eagles. And, of course, the sight of a minke whale gracefully arcing through the water, or an orca fin breaking through the waves, is unforgettable. Visit the Hebridean Whale and Dolphin Trust Discovery Centre to sign up for a summer Headland Watch trip along the award-winning Hebridean Whale Trail.

The lochside cabins are only accessible by boat, buggy or on foot

The architect-designed cabins offer seclusion and tranquillity

A far cry from roughing it

It's all about shifting down a few gears here: wild swimming, hiking, kayaking

Inverlonan: a luxury twist on the classic bothy experience

INVERLONAN

Bothies are simple refuges in isolated spots, traditionally used by shepherds and, more recently, mountain hikers. But, over on the west coast of Scotland, Inverlonan is reimagining the bothy experience. Set on a remote estate in Oban, the three architect-designed cabins offer the typical seclusion associated with this type of accommodation – with a luxury twist. Think cosy wood-burners, solar-powered lights, private decks, open firepits and outdoor pizza ovens. The interiors could be plucked from a design magazine; all local larch and glass. It's a far cry from roughing it. Peeking out from ancient oaks, the off-grid hideouts sit on the shore of Loch Nell in Oban and are only accessible by boat, buggy or on foot. The larder spills over with artisan produce grown on the owners' farm or sourced from local makers. It's all about slipping down a few gears here: long days spent wild swimming, kayaking, hiking and relaxing in this unplugged spot.

JURA

Twenty-eight miles long and eight wide, the long whale-shaped island of Jura is one of the wildest of the Inner Hebrides, its west coast inaccessible except to the dedicated walker. The distinctive Paps of Jura, so-called because of their breast--like shape, dominate every view off the west coast of Argyll. The island's name is thought to derive from the Norse *dyr-oe* (deer island) and, sure enough, the deer population of 6000 outnumbers the 190 or so humans 33 to 1. With just one road, tracing the east coast, and only one hotel, a few B&Bs and some self-catering cottages, Jura is a tranquil spot with great walking. In April 1946, Eric Blair (AKA George Orwell), moved to the remote north, where he wrote his final novel *1984*. Nearby, the Corryvreckan Whirlpool is thought to be caused by a rocky pinnacle 100ft below the sea, creating standing waves up to 15ft during gale-force winds. The place – *coire bhreacain* (speckled cauldron) in Gaelic – is shrouded in legend concerning *Cailleach* (Hag), the Celtic storm goddess. View it from Carraig Mhor, or take a boat trip from Seil.

The distinctive Paps of Jura

Boat tour to Corryvreckan Whirlpool

You're more likely to come across sheep than other tourists on Jura

The deer population outnumbers the humans 33 to 1 on Jura

The standing stones of Kilmartin Glen

Temple Wood stone circle

Achnabreac prehistoric rock art

Temple Wood, an ancient site in Kilmartin Glen

View from Dunadd Fort

KILMARTIN

Prehistoric sites are ten-a-penny in Scotland, though few rate as memorably as the one in Kilmartin Glen. Set in mid-Argyll countryside, an extraordinary two-mile-long linear cemetery comprises Neolithic and Bronze Age burial cairns, standing stones and circles, and cup and ring-marked rocks. It likely represents the successive burials of a local wealthy ruling family. Incredibly, there are thought to be 350 ancient monuments within a six-mile radius of Kilmartin. For the best views, scramble to the top of Dunadd Fort, on Mòine Mhór – the Great Moss, now a nature reserve. A modest but historically significant mound, Dunadd was once the seat of the Gaelic kings, Dal Riata. For an overview of the region's outstanding cultural landscape, visit the excellent Kilmartin Museum.

The thrilling first tee shot at Machrihanish Golf Club

The fairways are dictated by the original contours of the land

Machrihanish Dunes: a scenic backdrop for golf

A bell to signal golfers are moving on to the next tee

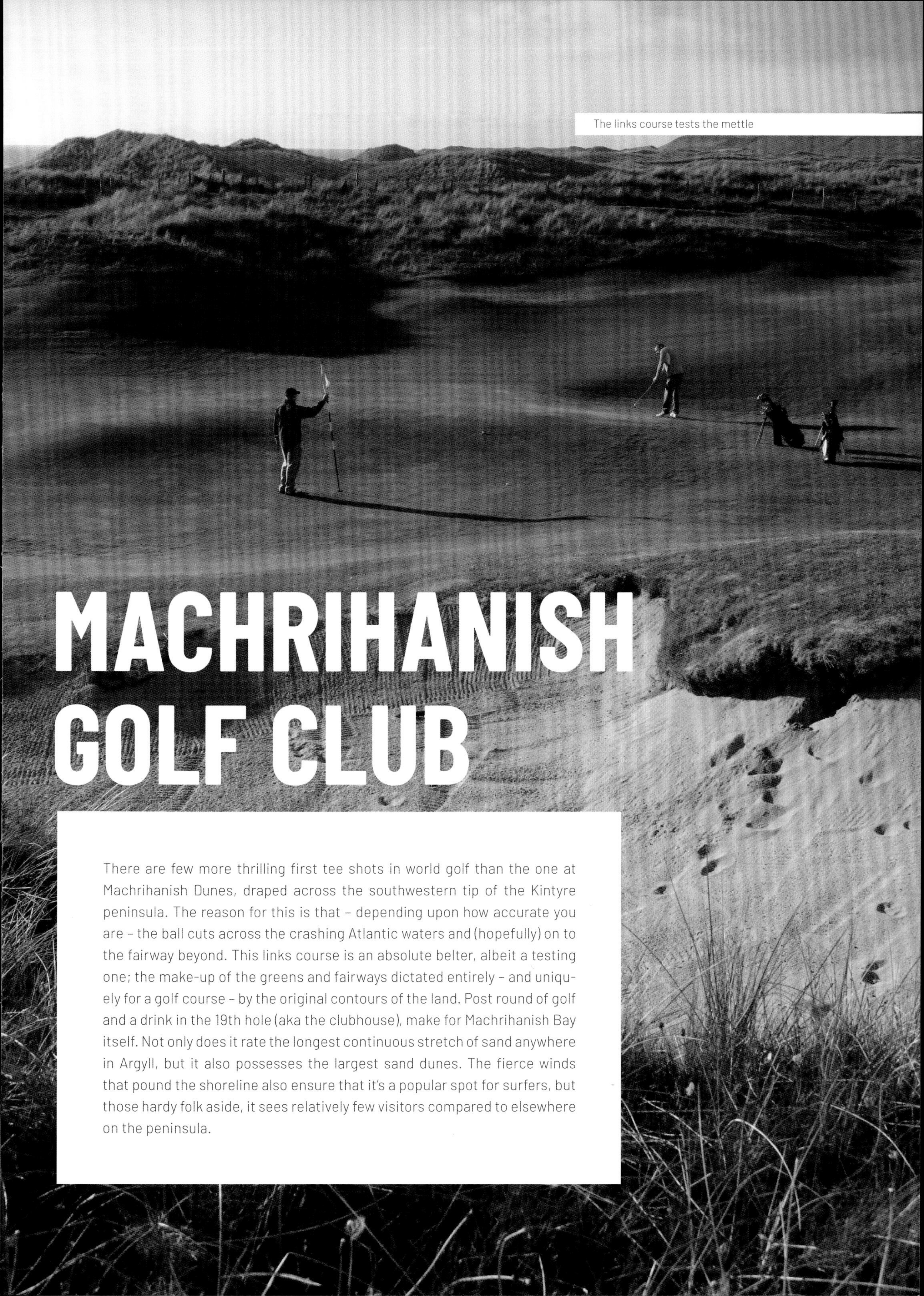

The links course tests the mettle

MACHRIHANISH GOLF CLUB

There are few more thrilling first tee shots in world golf than the one at Machrihanish Dunes, draped across the southwestern tip of the Kintyre peninsula. The reason for this is that – depending upon how accurate you are – the ball cuts across the crashing Atlantic waters and (hopefully) on to the fairway beyond. This links course is an absolute belter, albeit a testing one; the make-up of the greens and fairways dictated entirely – and uniquely for a golf course – by the original contours of the land. Post round of golf and a drink in the 19th hole (aka the clubhouse), make for Machrihanish Bay itself. Not only does it rate the longest continuous stretch of sand anywhere in Argyll, but it also possesses the largest sand dunes. The fierce winds that pound the shoreline also ensure that it's a popular spot for surfers, but those hardy folk aside, it sees relatively few visitors compared to elsewhere on the peninsula.

MOUNT STUART

The lovely Isle of Bute, accessed by ferry from Wemyss Bay, is generally a modest beach-holiday destination, within a pebble's throw of Glasgow. But all sense of modesty was chucked into the Firth of Clyde when the Marquess of Bute, an architect and eccentric, created Mount Stuart. The original family home was almost destroyed by fire in 1877 and the new abode, containing the surviving contents of the old, is a huge Italianate Gothic mansion adorned with lavish decoration. A railway line had to be specially created to haul the tons of shimmering white Carrara marble used for the construction of the Marble Chapel. Elsewhere, stained-glass windows depict the signs of the zodiac – the marquess had a penchant for mysticism – as well as images from the natural world: look out for a carved frog playing a lute, squirrels foraging in the dining room panelling and painted monkeys reading in the library.

The huge Italianate Gothic mansion is adorned with lavish decoration

The decadent Marble Hall

A railway line was specially created to haul the Carrara marble in for the chapel

Iona has been a focus of pilgrimage since Columba fled here in 563

Sunset at Iona

Iona Abbey cloisters

The clock-adorned abbey spire

PILGRIMAGE TRAIL

The tiny isle of Iona, off the southwest tip of Mull, has been a focus of pilgrimage since Columba fled here from Ireland in 563. He established a monastery, and it was from here that the sweeping conversion of the pagan Scots began. Follow in these footsteps, from rocky St Ronans Bay past the ruins of a fourteenth-century Augustinian nunnery to the Iona Heritage Centre, housed in a former manse. Stroll on to St Martin's Cross, with its fifteenth-century carvings, and continue on until you reach Iona Abbey. Due to Viking attacks, little remains of Columba's sixth-century settlement. But in 1200, Benedictine monks restored and in parts reconstructed the chapel, St Columba's Shrine and the abbey itself.

St Martin's Cross

TIREE

The most westerly of the Inner Hebridean isles, treeless Tiree rewards those who make the considerable effort to get here with distinctive architecture, incredible flora and fauna, and shimmering beaches. It also boasts more sunshine than any other place in Scotland – well, that's what the locals will tell you. Above all, though, the island is synonymous with surf. While Scotland has no shortage of amazing places to hit the waves, ask any surfer – wave, wind or kite – and they will tell you that Tiree is tops. The best months to surf are those either side of July and August, when the powerful offshore winds offer optimum conditions. The season climaxes in October when the world's finest surfers descend on the sands for the Tiree Wave Classic, the longest-running pro-surf competition in the calendar. It's an absolute blast, with much partying taking place alongside the serious business of the sport itself.

It's not just surfers who flock to Tiree's sandy beaches

Tiree is peppered with traditional crofts

Tiree Wave Classic

Lobster creel, a nod to Tobermory's fishing roots

The upper town offers great bay views

Whisky from Tobermory Distillery

Tours and tastings are available at Tobermory Distillery

TOBERMORY

Mull's chief town, Tobermory, at the northern tip of the island, is easily the most attractive fishing port on the west coast of Scotland, its clusters of brightly coloured houses and boats sheltering in a bay backed by a steep bluff. Founded in 1788 by the British Society for Encouraging Fisheries, it never really took off as a fishing port and only survived due to the steady influx of crofters evicted from other parts of the island during the Clearances. It is now the most important, and by far the most vibrant, settlement on Mull, and if you've got young kids, you'll instantly recognize it as the place where *Balamory* was filmed. The harbour – known as Main Street – is one long parade of candy-coloured hotels, guesthouses, restaurants and shops. The rest of the upper town, laid out on a classic grid plan, offers great views over the bay. Be sure to call by the Mull Aquarium, Europe's first catch-and-release aquarium, meaning all marine life (mostly caught by local divers and fishermen) is released in to the waters within four weeks, then pause for a dram in the Tobermory Distillery.

Tobermory's multicoloured harbour

TRESHNISH ISLES

Northwest of Staffa lie the Treshnish Isles, an archipelago of uninhabited volcanic islets, none more than a mile or two across. The most distinctive is Bac Mór, shaped like a Puritan's hat and popularly dubbed the Dutchman's Cap. Lunga, the largest island, is a summer nesting place for hundreds of seabirds, in particular guillemots, razorbills and puffins; the last of these are far and away the star attraction, and, for many, the main reason for visiting. It's also a major breeding ground for seals. From April to October several operators offer boat trips to the Treshnish Isles. The two most northerly islands, Cairn na Burgh More and Cairn na Burgh Beg, have remains of ruined castles, the first of which served as a lookout post for the Lords of the Isles and was last garrisoned in the Civil War; Cairn na Burgh Beg hasn't been occupied since the 1715 Jacobite uprising.

Atlantic puffins steal the show on Lunga

Lunga is a major breeding ground for seals

Sunrise over the Treshnish Isles

The Boathouse, Ulva's only café

ULVA

Located off the southwest of Mull, Ulva is a magical, time-stopped place that's almost lost in the fold of the map. For decades, this island of no cars, no shops, no postcards and no cheery tour guides, was home to only six residents, a shoreline café and two bothies (shelters), both 7km from the boat jetty. But rather than face further depopulation like so many Scottish islands, the locals took matters into their own hands, shaping a community buyout in 2018. Now, the Storas Ulbha cultural heritage centre is in the pipeline, alongside new accommodation, and this island time-capsule is in the throes of a renaissance. The rewards for visitors are sightings of Scotland's big five (golden eagles, red deer, otters, seals, harbour porpoise), closeness to nature, and peace. The Ulva Ferry runs in summer by demand only.

THE BOATHOUSE

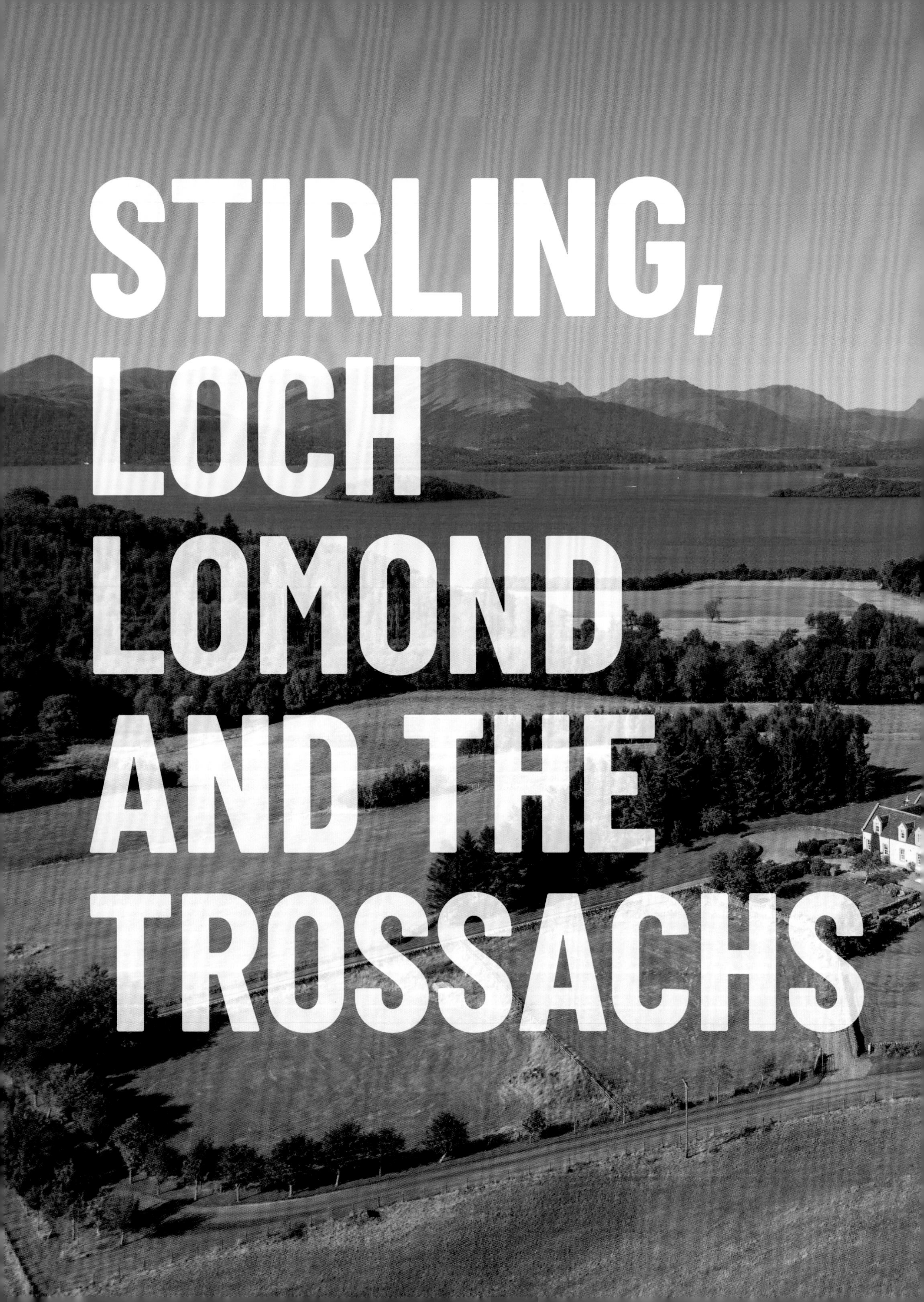
STIRLING, LOCH LOMOND AND THE TROSSACHS

ARGATY RED KITES

Twitchers, kids, wildlife fans... pretty much anyone will find a visit to Argaty Red Kites irresistible. Located just outside the handsome village of Doune, the working farm provides a feeding station for the once-persecuted red kites, whose russet-hued feathers, forked tails, serene floating motion and huge wingspan make them gratifyingly easy to identify. Argaty was involved in the reintroduction of red kites, which were hunted to near-extinction in the UK in the 1950s, and numbers have thankfully since recovered. Tucked in a hide, you can watch the birds' acrobatics as they swoop down to feed, while rangers give you lively background on the majestic creatures. You can also spot red squirrels, buzzards, peregrine falcons and kestrels. Not just an advocate for feathered friends, Argaty Red Kites also assisted in the relocation of a family of beavers, who were due to be culled in late 2021, to the farm. These wonderful creatures, known as nature's engineers, help reduce flooding and increase biodiversity. A second family joined them in early 2022, and these impressive rewilding achievements have put the centre on the conservation map.

Kites diving for food

Beavers are the latest addition to the farm

Red squirrel hides offer up-close sightings

Kites scrapping

INCHCAILLOCH

On the eastern shore of Loch Lomond, the tiny waterside settlement of Balmaha straddles the Highland Boundary Fault. If you stand on the viewpoint above the pier, you can see the fault line clearly marked by the series of woody islands that form giant stepping stones across the loch. The closest to the shore, Inchcailloch was extensively planted with oaks to provide bark for the local tanning industry. Now owned by the Scottish Natural Heritage, the forested speck is encircled by a two-mile nature trail, which passes the ruins of a fourteenth-century nunnery and associated burial ground, a picnic and camping site, and a sandy beach. Until the mid-seventeenth century parishioners on the far (western) shore of Loch Lomond used to row across to Inchcailloch for Sunday services at the church linked to the nunnery. Today, a small ferry carts visitors across the water, with departures on demand.

Inchcailloch is carpeted in bluebells in spring

Port of Menteith Church

Karma Lake of Menteith hotel

Fishing on the lake at sunset

Ruins of an Augustinian abbey on Inchmahome island

LAKE OF MENTEITH

Scotland has few more romantic spots than the Lake of Menteith. The only lake in the country – the rest of them are termed 'lochs' – sits just to the east of the mighty Trossachs. The hill and mountain views in all directions are sublime, as are the clear waters encircled by woodland. A good access point is the Karma Lake of Menteith hotel, which is also an excellent food stop. From here you can wander to the shore for a dip at one of the secluded stony beaches or, better still, catch the little ferry that nips across the lake to its uninhabited island, Inchmahome. Once on this tiny emerald speck, wander through the ancient woodland – the Spanish chestnuts date back to the 1500s – to the thirteenth-century ruins of an Augustinian abbey, still graceful despite its decline. Mary, Queen of Scots played here as a five-year-old – she was hidden on the island before being taken to France. Indeed, local legend says that the chestnut trees, with their leaning, twisted trunks, were planted by the small royal.

A motorboat ferry whisks visitors to Inchmahome Priory

LOCH LOMOND

The largest stretch of fresh water in Britain – 23 miles long and up to five wide – Loch Lomond is the epitome of Scottish scenic splendour, thanks in large part to the ballad that fondly recalls its "bonnie, bonnie banks". The Loch Lomond and the Trossachs National Park covers over seven hundred square miles of scenic territory from Loch Long in Cowal to Loch Earn and Loch Tay, on the southwest fringes of Perthshire. The centrepiece is undoubtedly Loch Lomond, and the most popular gateway is Balloch at the loch's southern tip. Very different in tone, the verdant eastern side of the loch, abutting the Trossachs, operates at a slower pace, with wooden ferryboats puttering out to tree-covered islands off the village of Balmaha. If you're looking for a relatively easy climb with an impressive view over Loch Lomond, start at Balmaha for the ascent of Conic Hill (1175ft), a two- to three-hour round-trip walk through forest and open hillside.

View from Conic Hill

Fishing boat on Loch Lomond

Explore Loch Lomond by pedal boat, canoe or bike

The *Maid of the Loch* paddle steamer at Balloch Pier

Stirling castle is poised on a rocky precipice

The sheer 250ft castle crag was first fortified in the Iron Age

View of Stirling from the top of the National Wallace Monument

Sculpture on the Prince's Walk

Stirling Castle sitting proud on Castle Hill

STIRLING CASTLE

Taking a winding walk up the lanes of the Old Town of Stirling is the best way to approach its wonderful castle, which sits proud and defensive on a high crag looking west towards the Trossach Mountains. The sheer 250ft castle crag was first fortified in the Iron Age, but the building you see today dates from the fifteenth and sixteenth centuries, the golden age of the city of Stirling, when it was the favourite residence of the Stuart monarchy. Highlights of the building, aside from sweeping battlement views, include its mighty Great Hall with a hammer-beam roof hewn from 35 oaks; the Stirling Heads, oak medallions carved with portraits of royal, Biblical and mythological figures; the tranquil Queen Anne Gardens; and the impressive palace tapestries, born out of a fourteen-year research and weaving project.

FIFE

Crail is rooted in its fishing heritage

Cobbled streets of Crail

Fishing boats bob in the harbour

Lobster creels on Crail Harbour

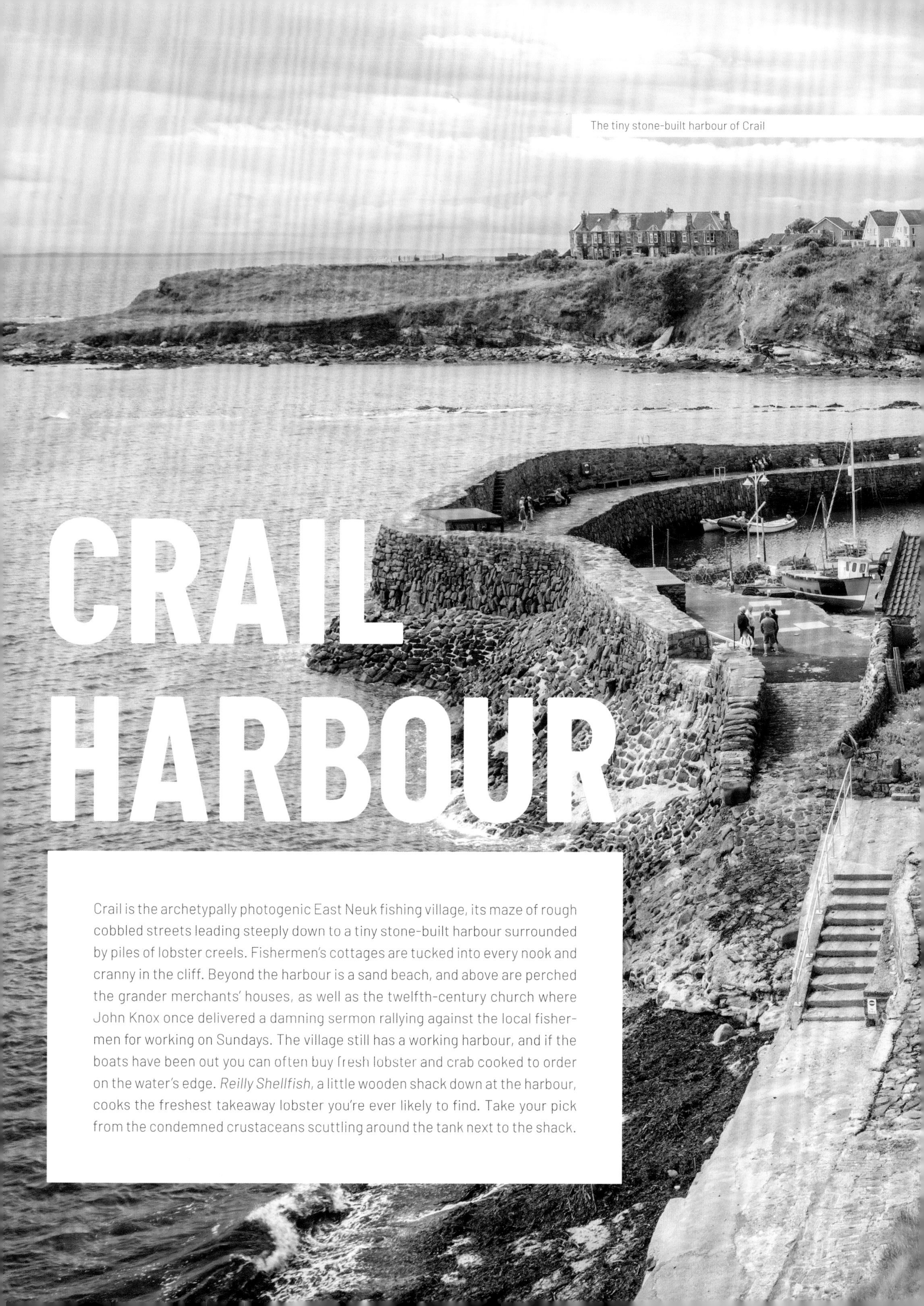

The tiny stone-built harbour of Crail

CRAIL HARBOUR

Crail is the archetypally photogenic East Neuk fishing village, its maze of rough cobbled streets leading steeply down to a tiny stone-built harbour surrounded by piles of lobster creels. Fishermen's cottages are tucked into every nook and cranny in the cliff. Beyond the harbour is a sand beach, and above are perched the grander merchants' houses, as well as the twelfth-century church where John Knox once delivered a damning sermon rallying against the local fishermen for working on Sundays. The village still has a working harbour, and if the boats have been out you can often buy fresh lobster and crab cooked to order on the water's edge. *Reilly Shellfish*, a little wooden shack down at the harbour, cooks the freshest takeaway lobster you're ever likely to find. Take your pick from the condemned crustaceans scuttling around the tank next to the shack.

The palace gardens are planted with herbs and vegetables of the period

Cobbled streets of Culross

Culross Palace

Remnants of Culross Abbey

CULROSS

The beautifully preserved seventeenth-century village of Culross on the Fife coast is a gem of a place, with cobbled streets, gabled houses and even its own palace and abbey. The presence of such grand buildings in such of an out-of-the-way spot is due to the village's early invention of undersea coal extraction. Wealthy merchant George Bruce built Culross Palace in the late 1700s: it's a rambling ochre-painted place with wood panelling, decorated ceilings and a garden planted with herbs and vegetables of the period. Up the hill, past rows of cottages with crow-stepped gables and plenty of intriguing passageways to lead you off course, you'll find the remnants of Culross Abbey. Founded by Cistercian monks on land given to the Church in 1217 by the earl of Fife, the nave of the original building is a ruin. The choir of the abbey became the parish church in 1633; a tenth-century Celtic cross in the north transept nods to the abbey's origins. Outside, the eighteenth-century gravestones are strikingly carved with symbols of the deceased person's occupation.

The beautifully preserved seventeenth-century cottages of Culross

DUNFERMLINE ABBEY AND PALACE

Dunfermline Abbey is a stone monolith from the Middle Ages. Queen Margaret began building a Benedictine priory in 1072 (still visible beneath the nave of the present church), and her son, David I, raised the priory to the rank of abbey the following century. In 1303, during the Wars of Independence, most of the monastic buildings were destroyed by the English King Edward I's troops. Robert the Bruce helped rebuild the abbey and when he died was buried here minus his heart, which was sent, unsuccessfully, on a pilgrimage to the Holy Land, only to be buried at Melrose Abbey. Inside, the stained glass is impressive, and the thick columns are carved with chevrons, spirals and arrowheads. The guesthouse of Queen Margaret's Benedictine monastery became the palace in the sixteenth century under James VI, who gave both it and the abbey to his consort, Queen Anne of Denmark. Charles I, the last monarch to be born in Scotland, entered the world here in 1600. Today, all that is left of the palace is a long sandstone facade: a striking silhouette against the sky at dusk.

Robert the Bruce helped rebuild the abbey and was buried here

All that remains of the palace is a long sandstone facade

Thick columns carved with chevrons, spirals and arrowheads

Stained-glass windows

FALKLAND PALACE

A hunting retreat to the Stewart kings for two hundred years, the construction of Falkland Palace began at the behest of James IV in 1500, and was completed by James V. Charles II stayed here in 1650 when he was in Scotland for his coronation, but after the Jacobite rising of 1715 and temporary occupation by Rob Roy the palace was abandoned, remaining so until the late nineteenth century when it was acquired by the third marquess of Bute. He restored the palace, and today it is a stunning example of early Renaissance architecture, with corbelled parapet, mullioned windows, round towers and massive walls. Inside there's a stately drawing room, a Chapel Royal (still used for Mass) and a Tapestry Gallery with seventeenth-century Flemish hangings. Outside, herbaceous borders line a pristine lawn. Look out for the high walls of the oldest real (or royal) tennis court in Britain – built in 1539 for James V and still in use.

Stained-glass windows in the Chapel Royal and Tapestry Gallery

Falkland Palace began life as a hunting retreat to the Stewart kings

The oldest real (or royal) tennis court in Britain – built in 1539 for James V

View of the Old Course from The Bridge restaurant

Portraits of the original hotel proprietor William Rusack and Old Tom Morris

The Old Course clubhouse

Guestrooms are opulent in style

The grand, honey-stoned building dates to the 1880s

RUSACKS ST ANDREWS

Set in a grand, honey-stoned 1880s building, Rusacks St Andrews cuts a fine figure on the landscape. Iconic views take in the Old Course's hallowed eighteenth fairway and Swilken Bridge and, beyond, the machair-backed dunes of West Sands and a swathe of blue sea. Inside, walls are hung with portraits of the original hotel proprietor William Rusack and Old Tom Morris – four-time winner of the Open and father to a son, likewise called Tom, who also won the Open four times. While the hotel is firmly geared towards the golf aficionado, it will also win over those with no interest in the sport. The excellent rooftop restaurant rustles up Scottish-leaning dishes using seasonal, local ingredients; think fresh oysters, lobster and Fife farm steaks. The compact city of St Andrews, with its cathedral, castle ruins and harbour, is an easy walk away.

West Sands

St Andrews

The iconic location in 1981 sports drama film *Chariots of Fire*

St Andrews Cathedral

East Sands, part of the Fife Coastal Path

ST ANDREWS' BEACHES

Though better known for its prestigious, ancient university (est. 1410) and world--class golf status, St Andrews also boasts two gorgeous sandy beaches. At the northern edge of the town is West Sands, immortalized in 1981 historical sports drama film *Chariots of Fire* as the spot where the Olympians run in slow motion, across the sand and through the surf, to a soundtrack by by Vangelis. Stretching for two miles and backed by dunes and fairways, it's still much loved by runners, strollers, sandcastle-makers and birdwatchers: you may spot skylarks, meadow pipits and sand buntings here, and possibly the rarer ringed plover. The more compact East Sands sits by the city's harbour. Part of the Fife Coastal Path, this similarly lovely golden swathe is popular not only with walkers but also surfers and sailing enthusiasts too.

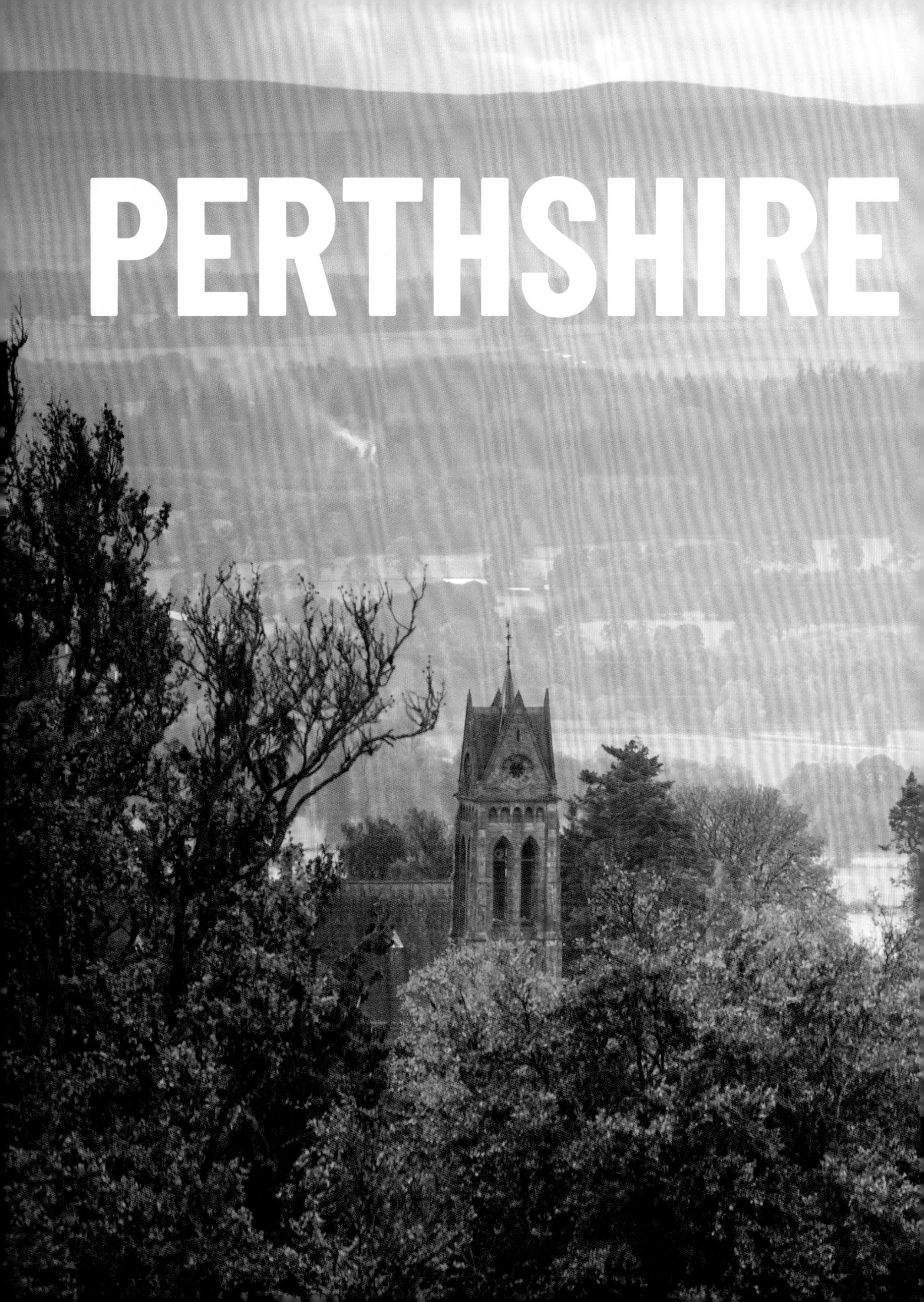
PERTHSHIRE

Atholl Highlanders

Sumptuous plasterwork in the dining room

Grand picture staircase

The Red Bedroom

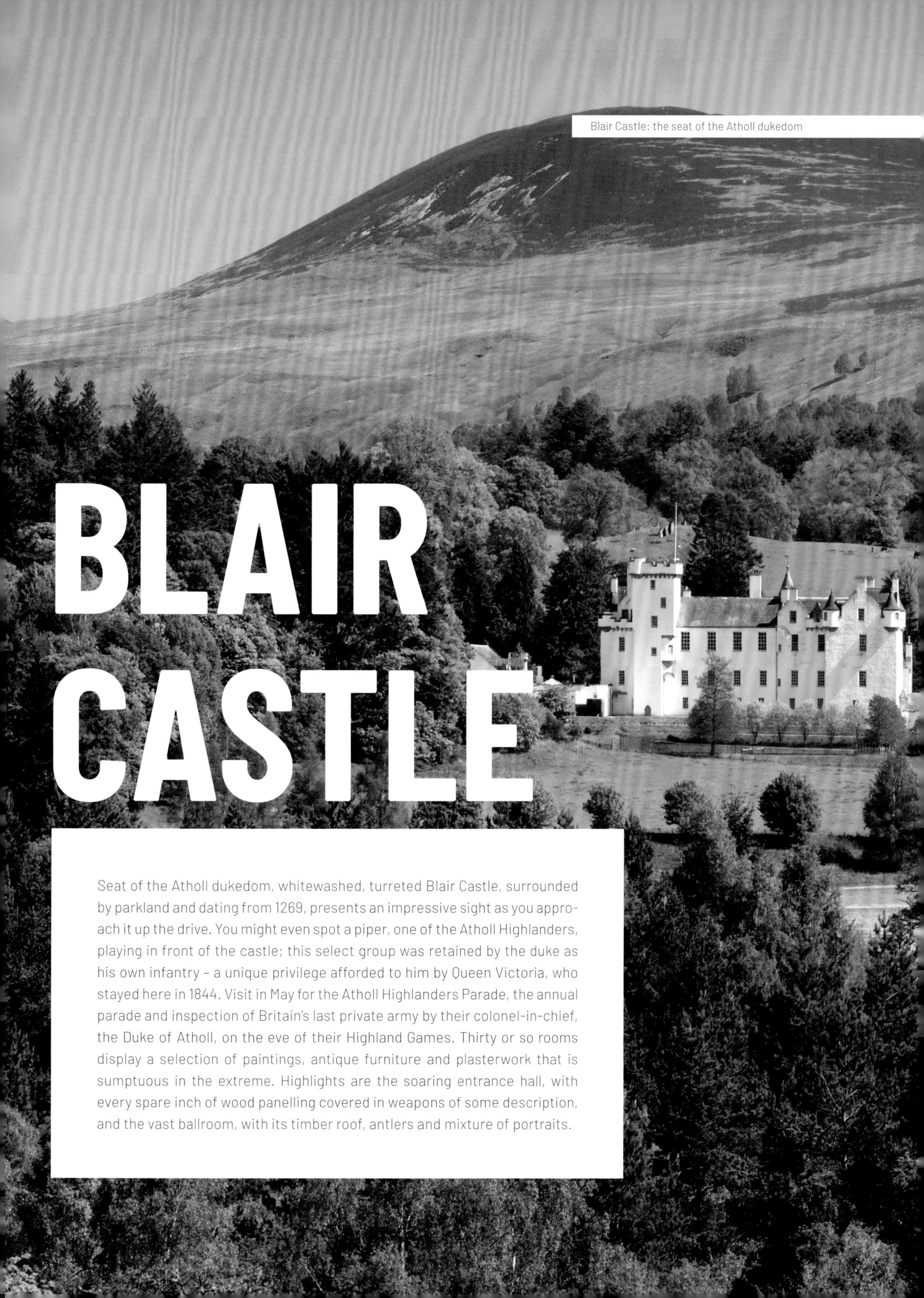

Blair Castle: the seat of the Atholl dukedom

BLAIR CASTLE

Seat of the Atholl dukedom, whitewashed, turreted Blair Castle, surrounded by parkland and dating from 1269, presents an impressive sight as you approach it up the drive. You might even spot a piper, one of the Atholl Highlanders, playing in front of the castle; this select group was retained by the duke as his own infantry – a unique privilege afforded to him by Queen Victoria, who stayed here in 1844. Visit in May for the Atholl Highlanders Parade, the annual parade and inspection of Britain's last private army by their colonel-in-chief, the Duke of Atholl, on the eve of their Highland Games. Thirty or so rooms display a selection of paintings, antique furniture and plasterwork that is sumptuous in the extreme. Highlights are the soaring entrance hall, with every spare inch of wood panelling covered in weapons of some description, and the vast ballroom, with its timber roof, antlers and mixture of portraits.

Italian marble statues punctuate the gardens

The castle itself is closed, but the garden alone warrants a visit

The garden in all its symmetrical glory

Drummond Castle Gardens is the finest attraction around Crieff

The terraced gardens are a peaceful haven

DRUMMOND CASTLE GARDENS

Of all the attractions around Crieff, most impressive are the magnificent Drummond Castle Gardens. The approach, up a splendid avenue of beech trees, is pretty enough, but by crossing the courtyard of the castle to the grand terrace you can view the garden in all its symmetrical glory. It was begun as early as 1630 (the date of the tall central sundial), though the design of the French/Italianate parterre is Victorian: it depicts a St Andrew's cross and incorporates other images associated with the Drummonds, including two crowns and the wavy motif found on the family crest. Italian marble statues punctuate the long lines of the cross, and the overall effect is of exceptional harmony and grace. Beyond the terraced gardens unfurls spacious parkland; a peaceful spot to walk. The castle itself is closed to visitors.

GLENEAGLES HOTEL

Iconic Gleneagles is famously home to three championship golf courses and enclosed in 850 acres of Perthshire countryside, an hour's drive from Edinburgh. The five-star hotel has welcomed leaders and celebrities from every corner of the globe. There's a plush spa and health club with two pools, sauna, steam room, hot tub, gym, indoor and outdoor tennis courts and a jam-packed programme of country pursuits, from horse riding to gundog training and falconry. If staying the night at the hotel is beyond your means, consider eating at the refreshingly unstuffy Andrew Fairlie at Gleneagles (three-course à la carte menu £115). It has two Michelin stars and is perhaps the finest restaurant in all of Scotland, serving up dynamic dishes like roast turbot with spiced verjus sauce.

The five-star hotel is set in 850 acres of Perthshire countryside

Artful mix of classic and contemporary

Falconry: one of the country pursuits available for guests

GLENTURRET

Dating back to 1775, Glenturret claims to be the oldest working whisky distillery in Scotland. Today it is still one of the more attractive, with low-slung whitewashed buildings set in woodland beside the gurgling River Turret. In 2021, a new fine-dining restaurant was opened in a converted pagoda, in part thanks to Lalique, the French glassmaker and Glenturret stakeholder that already has two Michelin-starred restaurants in Alsace and Bordeaux. Glasgow-born chef Mark Donald, of Number One at The Balmoral in Edinburgh, is the man behind the menu - inventive dishes may include locally sourced spring lamb, foraged white asparagus and morels, and haggis waffle. Whisky makes its way on to the dinner table (and not just in tumblers), weaved subtly into the likes of sourdough made with malted barley from the adjacent mill.

Glenturret claims to be the oldest working whisky distillery in Scotland

Tours at Glenturret Distillery

Rooftop whisky tasting

The wash still at Glenturret

RANNOCH MOOR

Rannoch Moor occupies roughly 150 square miles of uninhabited and uninhabitable peat bogs, lochs, heather hillocks, strewn lumps of granite and gnarled Caledonian pines, all 1000ft above sea level. Perhaps the most striking thing about the moor is its inaccessibility: one road, between Crianlarich and Glen Coe, skirts its western side, while another struggles west from Pitlochry to reach its eastern edge. The only regular transport here is the West Highland Railway, which stops at Rannoch and, a little to the north, Corrour, which has no road access at all - though it does have a great café. Corrour stole an unlikely scene in the film *Trainspotting* when the four central characters headed here for a taste of the great outdoors; a wooden SYHA hostel is located a mile away on the shores of Loch Ossian and can only be reached on foot. From Rannoch station, beside which is the isolated Moor of Rannoch Restaurant & Rooms, it's possible to catch the train to Corrour and walk the nine miles back; it's a longer slog to Glen Coe, the dramatic peaks of which poke up above the moor's western horizon. Determined hillwalkers will find a clutch of Munros around Corrour, including remote Ben Alder, 3765ft high above the forbidding shores of Loch Ericht.

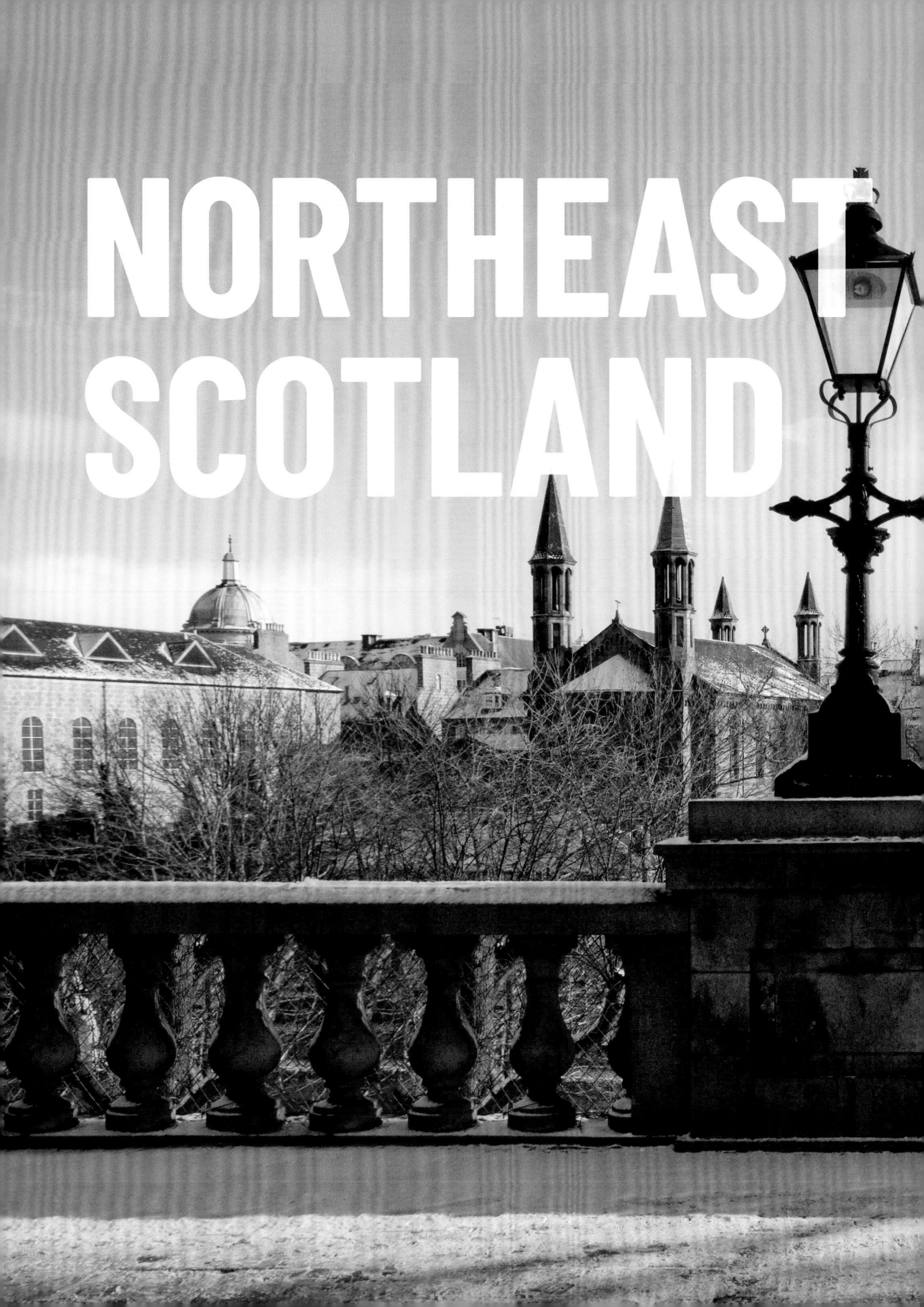
NORTHEAST
SCOTLAND

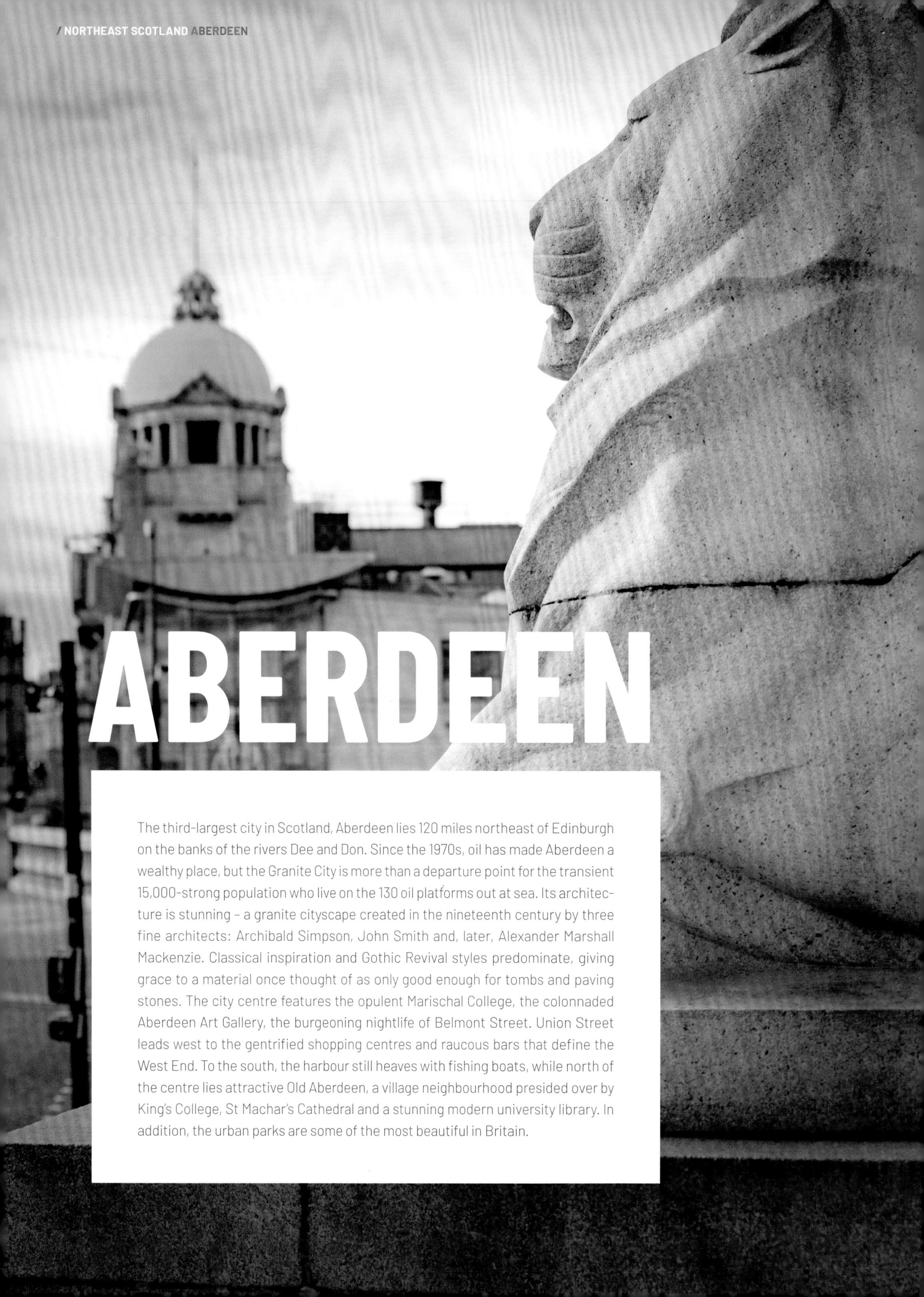

ABERDEEN

The third-largest city in Scotland, Aberdeen lies 120 miles northeast of Edinburgh on the banks of the rivers Dee and Don. Since the 1970s, oil has made Aberdeen a wealthy place, but the Granite City is more than a departure point for the transient 15,000-strong population who live on the 130 oil platforms out at sea. Its architecture is stunning – a granite cityscape created in the nineteenth century by three fine architects: Archibald Simpson, John Smith and, later, Alexander Marshall Mackenzie. Classical inspiration and Gothic Revival styles predominate, giving grace to a material once thought of as only good enough for tombs and paving stones. The city centre features the opulent Marischal College, the colonnaded Aberdeen Art Gallery, the burgeoning nightlife of Belmont Street. Union Street leads west to the gentrified shopping centres and raucous bars that define the West End. To the south, the harbour still heaves with fishing boats, while north of the centre lies attractive Old Aberdeen, a village neighbourhood presided over by King's College, St Machar's Cathedral and a stunning modern university library. In addition, the urban parks are some of the most beautiful in Britain.

Provost Skene's House

Marischal College

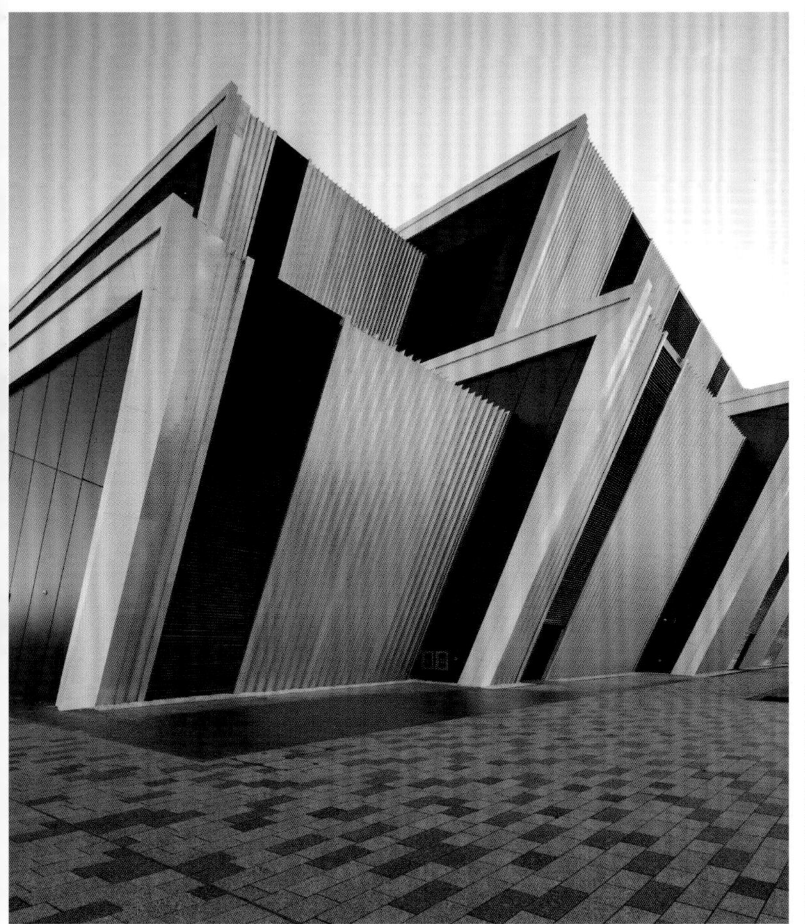
P&J Live, a modern events space

Aberdeen is famed for its stunning architecture

Fishing boats in Arbroath Harbour

Rick Stein is a big fan of M & M Spink

The Arbroath smokie: line-caught haddock, smoke-cured over smouldering oak chips

Signal Tower Museum

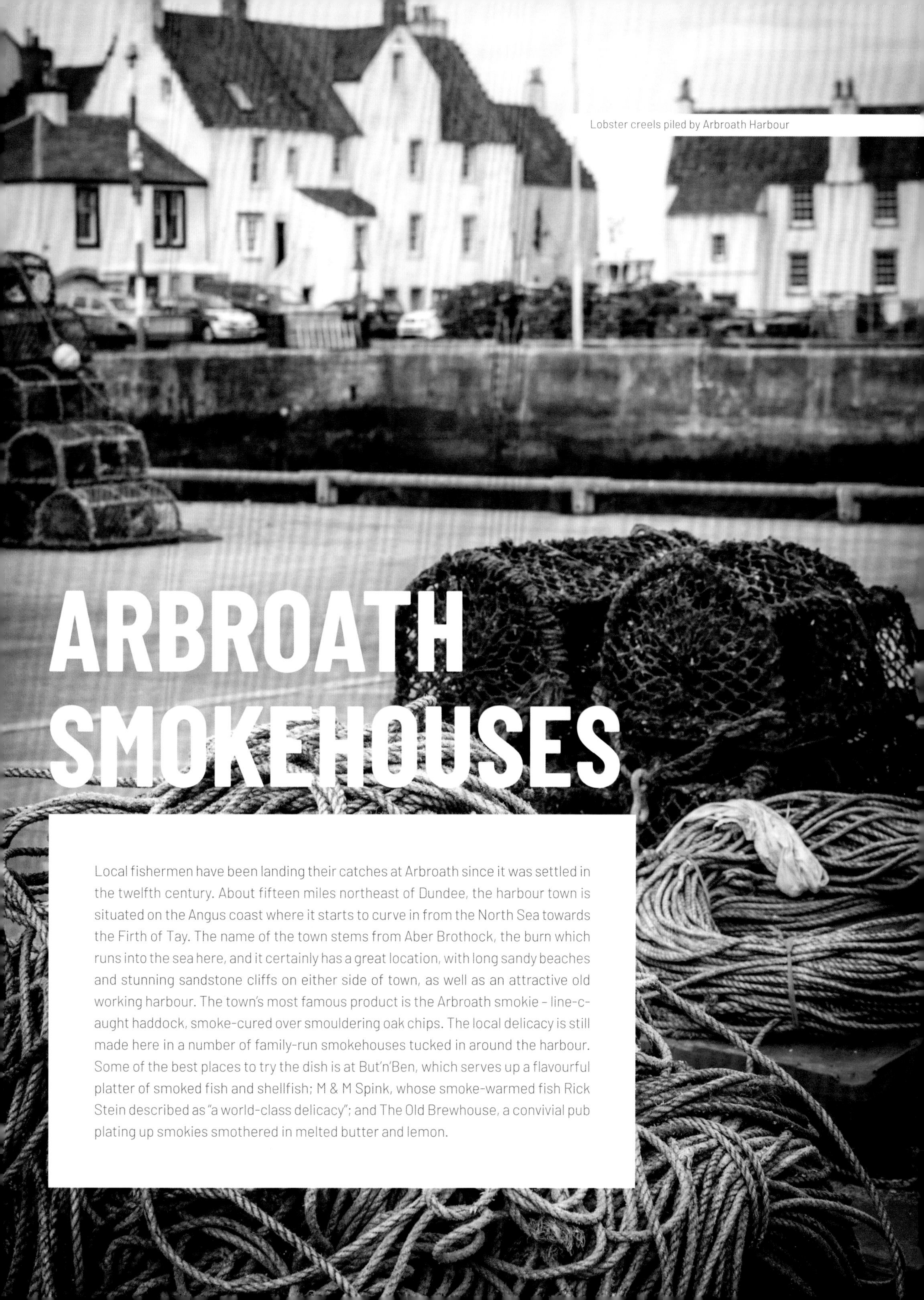

Lobster creels piled by Arbroath Harbour

ARBROATH SMOKEHOUSES

Local fishermen have been landing their catches at Arbroath since it was settled in the twelfth century. About fifteen miles northeast of Dundee, the harbour town is situated on the Angus coast where it starts to curve in from the North Sea towards the Firth of Tay. The name of the town stems from Aber Brothock, the burn which runs into the sea here, and it certainly has a great location, with long sandy beaches and stunning sandstone cliffs on either side of town, as well as an attractive old working harbour. The town's most famous product is the Arbroath smokie – line-caught haddock, smoke-cured over smouldering oak chips. The local delicacy is still made here in a number of family-run smokehouses tucked in around the harbour. Some of the best places to try the dish is at But'n'Ben, which serves up a flavourful platter of smoked fish and shellfish; M & M Spink, whose smoke-warmed fish Rick Stein described as "a world-class delicacy"; and The Old Brewhouse, a convivial pub plating up smokies smothered in melted butter and lemon.

The filming location for Zeffirelli's film version of *Hamlet*

DUNNOTTAR CASTLE

One of Scotland's finest ruined castles, Dunnottar Castle is a huge ninth-century fortress set on a three-sided sheer cliff jutting into the sea – a location striking enough to be chosen as the backdrop for Zeffirelli's film version of *Hamlet*. Once the principal fortress of the northeast, the mainly fifteenth- and sixteenth-century ruins are worth a good root around, and there are many dramatic views out to the crashing sea. Siege and bloodstained drama splatter the castle's past: in 1297 the whole English Plantagenet garrison was burnt alive here by William Wallace, while one of the more gruesome tales from the castle's history tells of the imprisonment and torture of 122 men and 45 women Covenanters in 1685 – an event, as it says on the Covenanters' Stone in the churchyard, "whose dark shadow is for evermore flung athwart the Castled Rock".

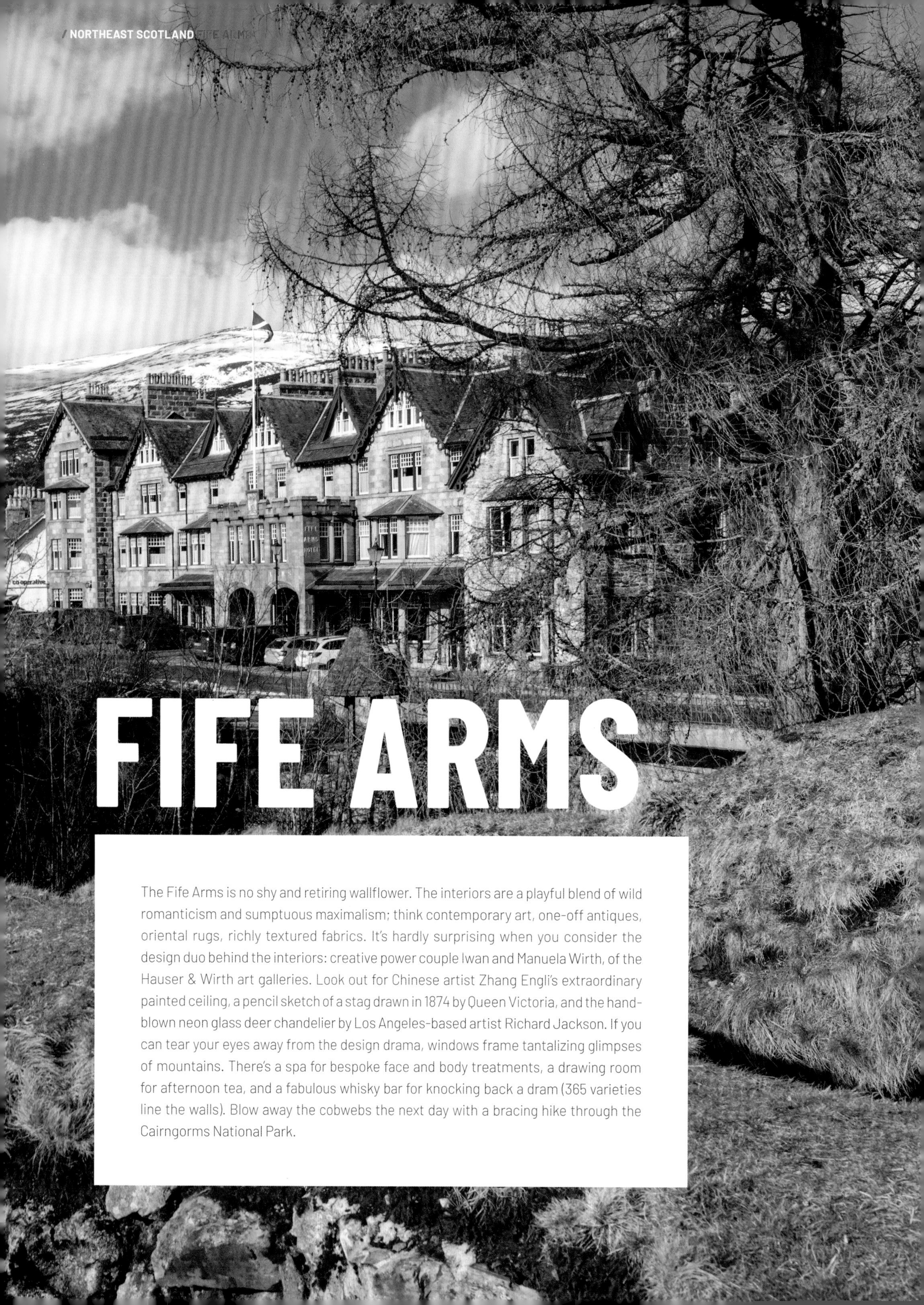

FIFE ARMS

The Fife Arms is no shy and retiring wallflower. The interiors are a playful blend of wild romanticism and sumptuous maximalism; think contemporary art, one-off antiques, oriental rugs, richly textured fabrics. It's hardly surprising when you consider the design duo behind the interiors: creative power couple Iwan and Manuela Wirth, of the Hauser & Wirth art galleries. Look out for Chinese artist Zhang Engli's extraordinary painted ceiling, a pencil sketch of a stag drawn in 1874 by Queen Victoria, and the hand-blown neon glass deer chandelier by Los Angeles-based artist Richard Jackson. If you can tear your eyes away from the design drama, windows frame tantalizing glimpses of mountains. There's a spa for bespoke face and body treatments, a drawing room for afternoon tea, and a fabulous whisky bar for knocking back a dram (365 varieties line the walls). Blow away the cobwebs the next day with a bracing hike through the Cairngorms National Park.

Design power couple Iwan and Manuela Wirth, of the Hauser & Wirth art galleries, are behind the interiors

The India Suite

Interiors are a playful mix of wild romanticism and sumptuous maximalism

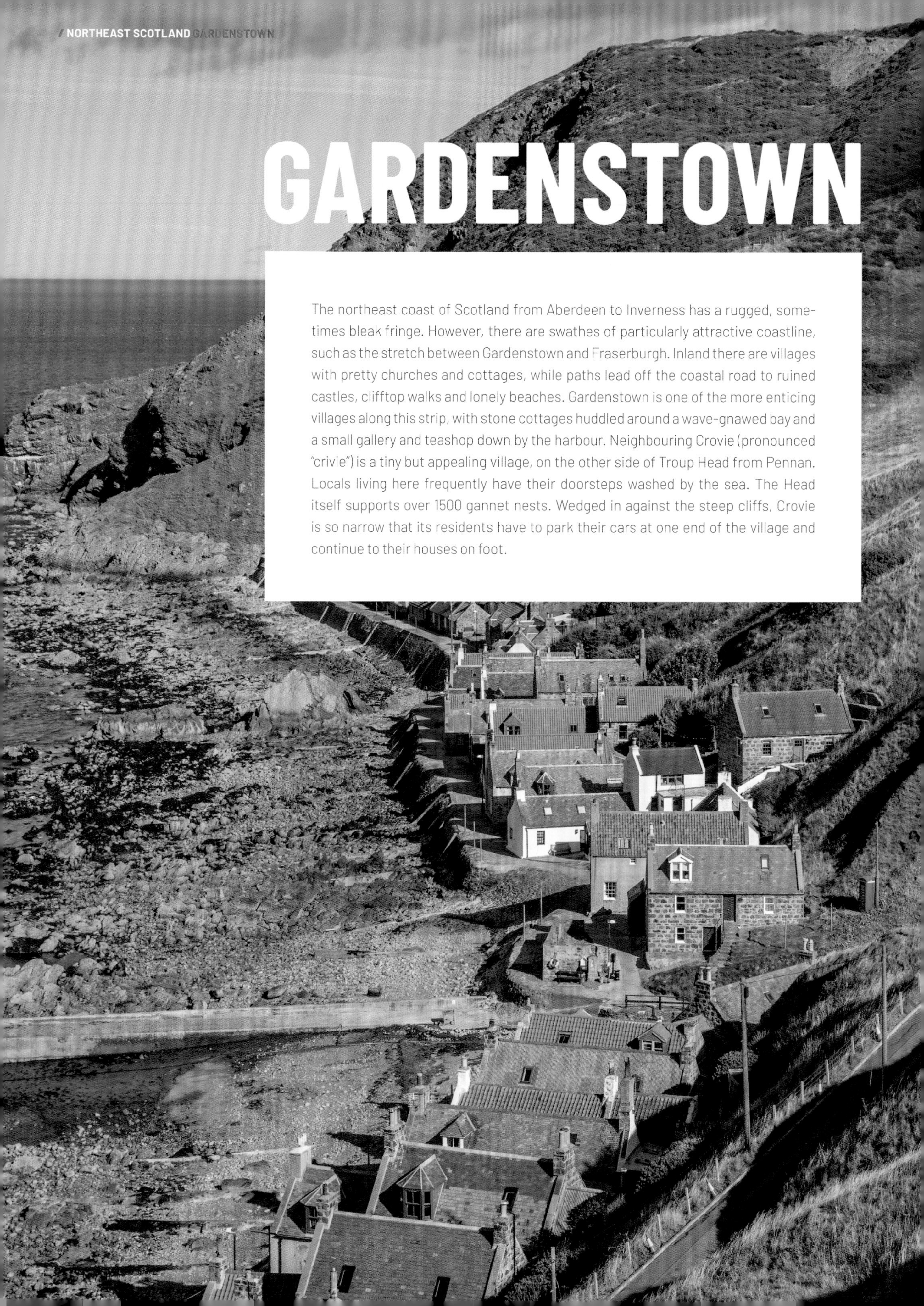

GARDENSTOWN

The northeast coast of Scotland from Aberdeen to Inverness has a rugged, sometimes bleak fringe. However, there are swathes of particularly attractive coastline, such as the stretch between Gardenstown and Fraserburgh. Inland there are villages with pretty churches and cottages, while paths lead off the coastal road to ruined castles, clifftop walks and lonely beaches. Gardenstown is one of the more enticing villages along this strip, with stone cottages huddled around a wave-gnawed bay and a small gallery and teashop down by the harbour. Neighbouring Crovie (pronounced "crivie") is a tiny but appealing village, on the other side of Troup Head from Pennan. Locals living here frequently have their doorsteps washed by the sea. The Head itself supports over 1500 gannet nests. Wedged in against the steep cliffs, Crovie is so narrow that its residents have to park their cars at one end of the village and continue to their houses on foot.

Gardenstown Harbour

Locals living in Crovie frequently have their doorsteps washed by the sea

The tiny cottages of Crovie hook around Gamrie Bay

V&A DUNDEE

In the nineteenth century Dundee was Britain's main processor of jute, which earned the city the tag "Juteopolis". The decline of manufacturing wasn't kind to the 145,000-strong population, who are still living with its effects. However, regeneration is today's big buzzword, with some drawing comparisons with Glasgow's reinvention in the 1980s and 1990s. A major star of the cultural scene is the V&A Dundee, a waterfront design museum in a ship-like modern building, designed by Japanese architect Kengo Kuma as a homage to the city's shipping heritage and rugged rock-strewn coastline. The two upended stone-clad pyramid are unflinchingly modern, and provide an interesting foil to the lofty masts of the neighbouring *Discovery* vessel. The main attraction is the (free) Scottish Design Galleries, whose highlight is a brilliant reconstruction of Charles Rennie Mackintosh's Ingram Street Tearooms. Other exhibits celebrate the country's painters, fashionistas and illustrators, including the creator of Dundee's own cartoon hero Dennis the Menace. Look out for an ornate panel fragment from the Titanic, a winged Cartier headdress studded with diamonds, and Natalie Portman's *Star Wars* costume.

Dundee waterfront

Dennis the Menace, Dundee's own cartoon hero

The V&A Dundee is a leading light in the city's cultural renaissance

Scottish Design Galleries

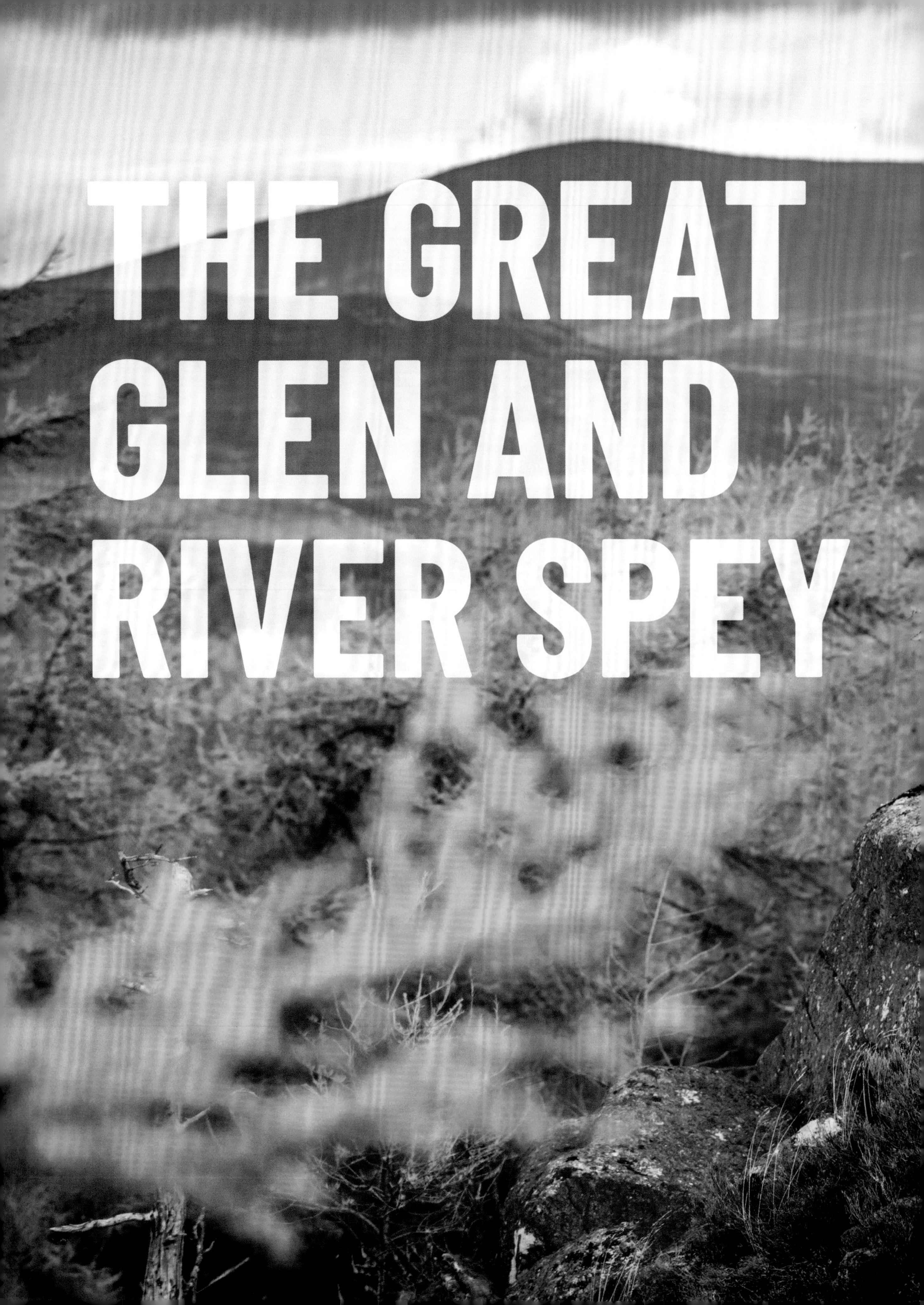
THE GREAT
GLEN AND
RIVER SPEY

CAIRNGORMS

The Cairngorms National Park covers almost 1750 square miles – the biggest in Britain. It incorporates the Cairngorms massif, the largest mountainscape in the UK and the only sizeable plateau in the country over 2500ft. The name comes from the Gaelic *An Carm Gorm*, meaning "the blue hill" after the blueish-tinged stones found in the area. The park is home to a quarter of Scotland's native woodland and a quarter of the UK's threatened wildlife species; the tracts of ancient Caledonian forest at Rothiemurchus are even home to red squirrels. Aviemore and the surrounding area are regarded as the main point of entry, particularly for those planning outdoor activities, but it's also possible to access the park from Perthshire as well as Deeside and Donside in Aberdeenshire. Crossing the range is a challenge: by road the only connection is the A939 from Tomintoul to Cock Bridge, often impassable in winter due to snow. On foot the only way to avoid the high peaks is to follow the old cattle drovers' route called the Lairig Ghru, a very long day's walk between Inverdruie at the edge of Rothiemurchus and the Linn of Dee, near Inverey.

Braemar village in Cairngorms National Park

Cairngorm Ski Resort

The ancient Caledonian forest at Rothiemurchus

Reindeer in the Cairngorms National Park

Chanonry Point at sunrise

CHANONRY POINT

The west coast of Scotland may have its whales, but over on the east is one of the best dolphin-spotting sites in all of Europe: Chanonry Point. Usually, when seeking out Scotland's magnificent wildlife, be it pine martens, white--tailed eagles or red deer stags, there are few guarantees. However, as the Moray Firth is home to the only resident bottlenose dolphin population in the north of Britain - there are thought to be around 200 here - sightings from the peninsula at the tip of the Black Isle are nailed on. Every day, come rain or shine, hundreds of excitable onlookers gather down by the lighthouse to catch a glimpse of these enchanting animals as they fish and frolic in the strong offshore currents. Although the pod is present year-round, the best time to see them is late spring or early summer when they come closer to shore to hunt salmon. Not only that, but you'll likely see porpoises and seals, and the occasional otter too. Do though check the tide times before setting off - you won't want to miss out.

Glen Coe is a skiing hotspot

Blackrock Cottage

A lonely road through Glen Etive

Kingshouse Hotel

GLEN COE

Breathtakingly beautiful Glen Coe ("Valley of Weeping"), sixteen miles south of Fort William, is a spectacular mountain valley between forbidding peaks, their conical tops often wreathed in cloud. Not just a place of dramatic beauty, Glen Coe is also rooted in high historical drama. In 1692 this was the site of a terrible government massacre, aimed to supress the supposedly lawless MacDonald clan. Campbell of Glenlyon was ordered to billet his soldiers with the MacDonalds of Glen Coe, and the soldiers received ten days of warm Highland hospitality from the clan. Then the soldiers turned on their hosts, killing more than forty people and causing over three hundred to flee into a February blizzard. The National Trust's eco-friendly visitor centre in the glen outlines this troubling story and its repercussions, as well as giving guidance on outstanding walks in the area. There are also interesting exhibits on ecology and conservation issues. Glencoe village is a handy base, where the heather-roofed Glencoe Folk Museum brings eighteenth-century crofting to vivid life.

River Coupall falls

LOCH NESS

Loch Ness is one of the most important stomping grounds in the Scottish Highlands. Though it is best known for the long-necked cryptid lurking in its depths, there is so much more to the loch than Nessie-chasing tours. For starters, it's a hiker's paradise, where pine-skirted mountains plunge into mirror-clear waters. Scramble up Meall Fuar-mhonaidh, Loch Ness' highest hill at 699m, or tackle the corkscrew route between Foyers and Dores on the lesser-trodden eastern shore. Test your mettle on the Great Glen Way or South Loch Ness Trail; together, they form the Loch Ness 360° Trail, a 106km-long circuit that takes three to six days to hike or bike. Beyond the toothy ramparts of Urquhart Castle, Fort Augustus is the start of the 19th-century Caledonian Canal, a 96km hand-dug waterway that leads budding houseboat captains south to Corpach near Fort William.

Nessie-chasing tours are popular on Loch Ness

Suidhe Viewpoint offers excellent loch views

Fort Augustus is the start of the 19th-century Caledonian Canal

Speyside Way

Whisky barrells at the Speyside Cooperage

Whisky tasting

Cragganmore Distillery

Glenlivet distillery

SPEYSIDE WHISKY TRAIL

There are more distilleries concentrated in the Speyside "whisky triangle" – a small area stretching from Craigellachie, down towards Tomintoul in the south and east to Huntly – than in any other part of Scotland. Scotland's malt whisky capital, Dufftown boasts no fewer than nine distilleries and is a popular base for a tour of whisky country. Fewer visitors venture to the more remote glens, such as Glenlivet, which push higher up towards the Cairngorms, nestled into which is Britain's highest village, Tomintoul. The 65 mile-long Speyside Way, with its beguiling blend of mountains, river, wildlife and whisky, is fast establishing itself as an alternative to the West Highland and Southern Upland long-distance footpaths. Starting at Buckie on the Moray Firth coast, it follows the River Spey from Spey Bay south to Aviemore, with branches linking it to Dufftown and Tomintoul. The route is a five- to seven-day expedition, but for shorter walks or cycling trips head to the stretch between Craigellachie and Glenlivet; the Glenfiddich, Glenlivet, Macallan and Cardhu distilleries all lie directly on or close to the route.

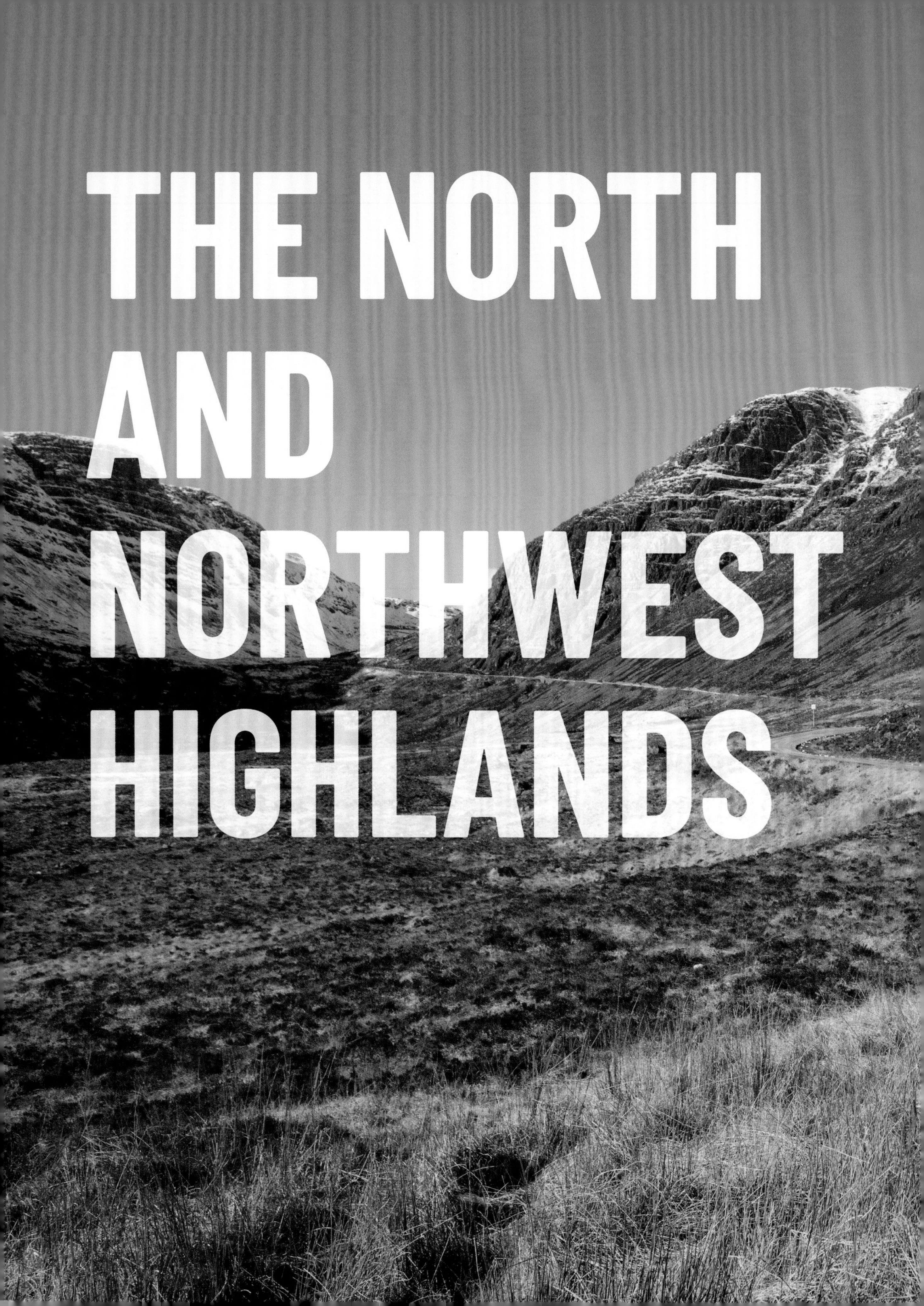

THE NORTH AND NORTHWEST HIGHLANDS

PASSING
PLACE

ARDNAMURCHAN

The most westerly point on the British mainland, Ardnamurchan is as remote as it is inspiring, with its endless sea vistas and empty beaches. The gateway to the region is the former lead-mining village of Strontian, from where a mostly single-track road weaves its way all along the southern shore, which itself bounds the northern rim of Loch Sunart, the longest sea loch in the country. It is unquestionably one of the loveliest drives in all of Scotland. But it's not one you can, or should, rush; not only does this drive necessitate patience, but there are diversions aplenty, such as the engaging Ardnamurchan Natural History Visitor Centre. The best bit, however, is Ardnamurchan Point, crowned by a splendid lighthouse designed by Alan Stevenson (uncle of Robert Louis) and, a few miles north of here, the magnificent belt of bleached white sand that is Sanna Bay. From here savour fantastic views across to the Small Isles, best enjoyed at sunset.

Loch Sunart

Ardnamurchan, the most westerly point on the British mainland

Ardnamurchan Lighthouse

Sanna Bay

Bealach na Bà (Pass of the Cattle) is said to be the highest mountain pass in Britain

Heavy snow over the pass

The road is deceptively straightforward on the approach from Tornapress

Highland cattle on the Applecross peninsula

BEALACH NA BÀ

It's said that the Bealach na Bà (Pass of the Cattle) on the Applecross peninsula is the highest mountain pass in Britain, with an ascent that rises 2054ft from almost sea level. At any rate, it's certainly the most spectacular. Approaching from Tornapress, just north of Lake Kishorn – where signs ominously warn against driving the route in larger vehicles – the road begins in fairly routine fashion. Then the gradient suddenly increases (it reaches twenty percent at its steepest section) and the curves become ever more sinuous, sculpted by a series of dramatic hairpin bends, all the while shadowed by an almighty tower of rock. For the truly fit, and possibly foolish, there's only one way to tackle the pass and that's by bike; indeed, the ascent is frequently rated as the toughest climb in Britain. However you decide to make the trip, the views at the top (2054ft) are simply stunning. On a clear day, spectacular panoramas stretch across to Skye and Raasay. Once at the summit you can relax in the knowledge that it's all downhill from here, unless you've got to cycle all the way back from the other side, of course.

Bealach na Bà passes over the Russell Burn river

CAPE WRATH

Closer to Iceland than to London, the forebodingly named Cape Wrath at the northwestern tip of the Scottish mainland is the definition of remote. This is nature at is most elemental, the kind of place where you half-expect to see a Viking warship glide into view – the windswept promontory does, after all, take its name from the Norse word *hvarf*, meaning 'turning place'. The most satisfying way to get here – the only way, in fact, unless you take the foot-passenger ferry from Keoldale then a minibus for 14 miles – is on foot from Sandwood Bay (full-day hike). However you get here, the rewards are immense, from the lonesome lighthouse built by Robert Louis Stevenson to the highest sea cliffs in Britain. Incredible views sweep northeast to Orkney and west to the Outer Hebrides. If it's solitude you're after, then this wild place takes some beating.

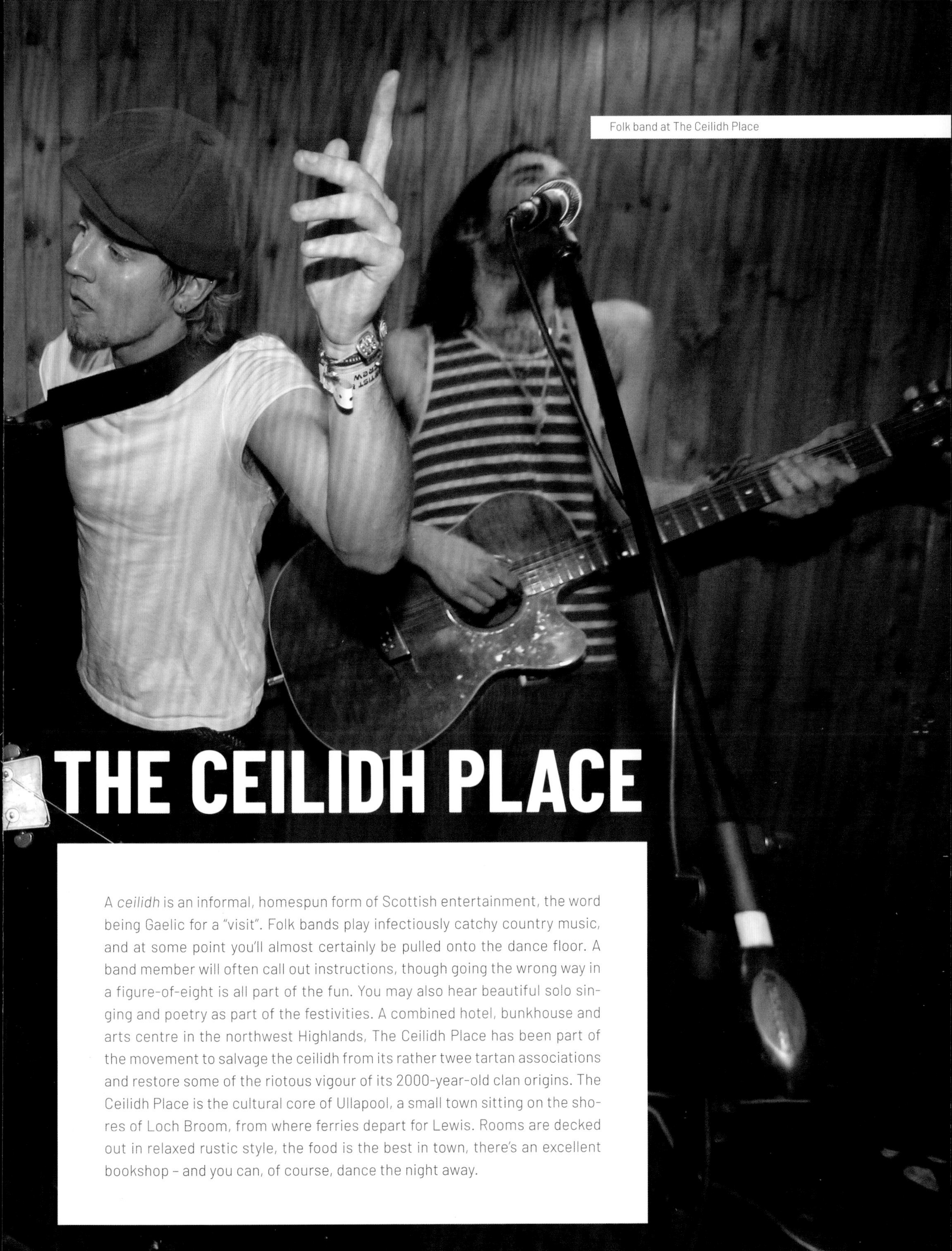

Folk band at The Ceilidh Place

THE CEILIDH PLACE

A *ceilidh* is an informal, homespun form of Scottish entertainment, the word being Gaelic for a "visit". Folk bands play infectiously catchy country music, and at some point you'll almost certainly be pulled onto the dance floor. A band member will often call out instructions, though going the wrong way in a figure-of-eight is all part of the fun. You may also hear beautiful solo singing and poetry as part of the festivities. A combined hotel, bunkhouse and arts centre in the northwest Highlands, The Ceilidh Place has been part of the movement to salvage the ceilidh from its rather twee tartan associations and restore some of the riotous vigour of its 2000-year-old clan origins. The Ceilidh Place is the cultural core of Ullapool, a small town sitting on the shores of Loch Broom, from where ferries depart for Lewis. Rooms are decked out in relaxed rustic style, the food is the best in town, there's an excellent bookshop – and you can, of course, dance the night away.

Set right on the shorefront of Loch Moidart, Tioram Cottage

Bedroom of The Bothy

The Artist Studio

The south shore

Coastline

EILEAN SHONA

You might have been to Scotland's northwest Highlands before, but there really is nothing to compare to Eilean Shona. It's a private, car-free island; a tidal Loch Moidart skerry cast off the Ardnamurchan peninsula, but a place more akin to a lost world of adventures where the stag-topped hills are bordered by Indian Ocean-esque beaches. *Peter Pan* author J.M. Barrie holidayed here - prompting plenty of hat tips to Neverland - and the sense of having a Lost Boys caper is palpable. There is wild swimming and crabbing off the pontoon, but also eagle-watching, seal-spotting, hill-climbing, kayaking, picnicking, campfire-building, and art classes. Ask the island stewards and they'll happily give you a quad-bike tour along a coast framed by fudgy sands and cornflower-blue seas. Even more appealing are the island's nine secluded, self-catering Hebridean cottages, all of which are scattered to every point of the compass.

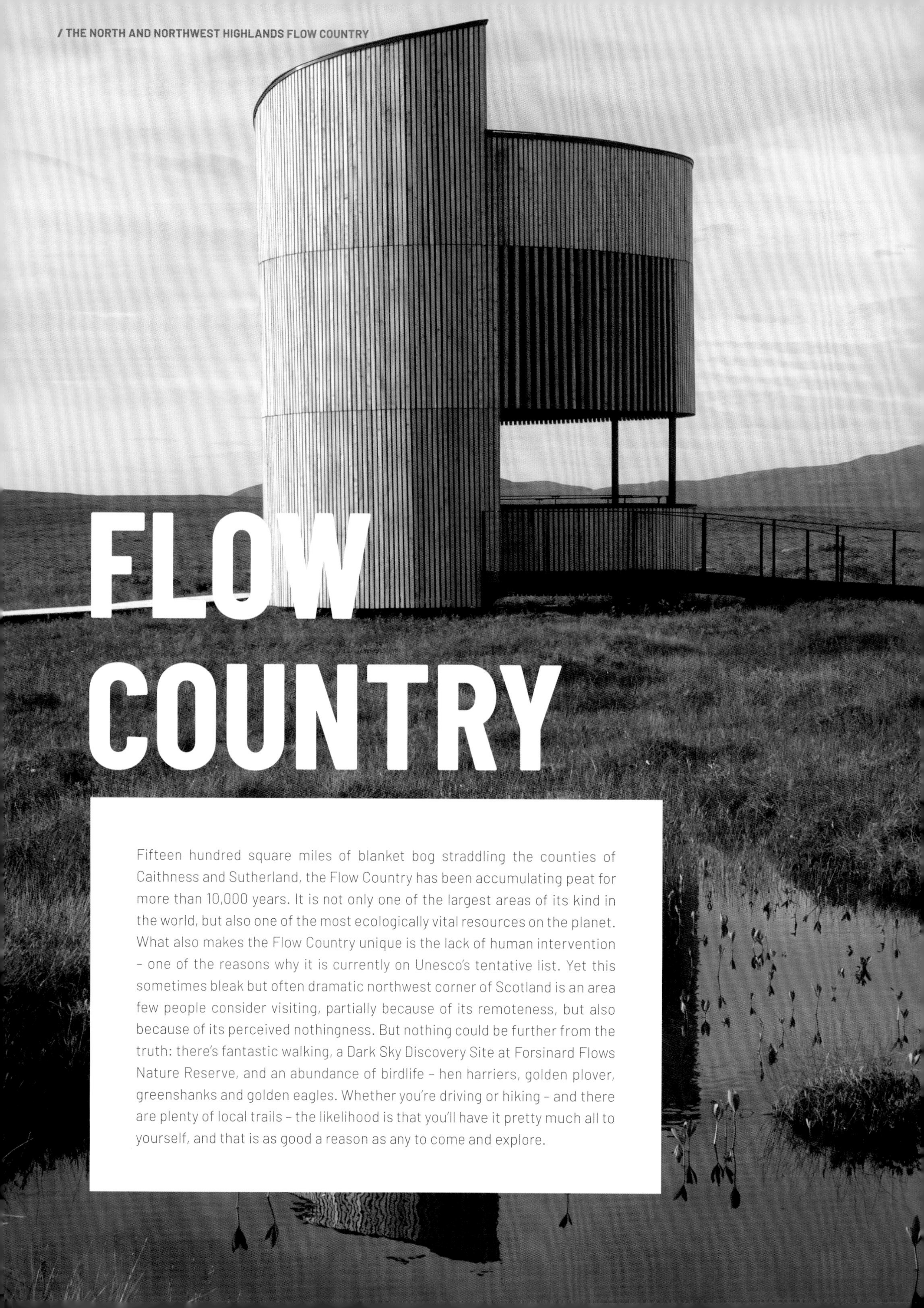

FLOW COUNTRY

Fifteen hundred square miles of blanket bog straddling the counties of Caithness and Sutherland, the Flow Country has been accumulating peat for more than 10,000 years. It is not only one of the largest areas of its kind in the world, but also one of the most ecologically vital resources on the planet. What also makes the Flow Country unique is the lack of human intervention – one of the reasons why it is currently on Unesco's tentative list. Yet this sometimes bleak but often dramatic northwest corner of Scotland is an area few people consider visiting, partially because of its remoteness, but also because of its perceived nothingness. But nothing could be further from the truth: there's fantastic walking, a Dark Sky Discovery Site at Forsinard Flows Nature Reserve, and an abundance of birdlife – hen harriers, golden plover, greenshanks and golden eagles. Whether you're driving or hiking – and there are plenty of local trails – the likelihood is that you'll have it pretty much all to yourself, and that is as good a reason as any to come and explore.

Forsinard Flows Nature Reserve

Dark Sky Discovery Site at Forsinard Flows

You're more likely to come across sheep than people in Flow Country

The fertile plains of Flow Country

The trail takes in the undulating landscape of the Highlands

GREAT NORTH TRAIL

The UK's most exciting new long-distance cycle route may begin in the Peak District but the greater length of its itinerary lies in Scotland, running from Kielder Forest by the border all the way to Cape Wrath and John O'Groats. Launched in 2019, the Great North Trail is groundbreaking in that it plots an almost entirely off-main-road course. In fact, the route ingeniously avoids traffic for the most part, instead taking in rough hill paths, disused railway lines, drove roads, old military roads, city cycle paths and canal towpaths as well as minor and single-track roads. Sure, this entails the occasional doubling back on yourself, but it neatly swerves the dread of A-roads up ahead, with only fresh air, wildlife and stunning scenery for company. The trail is a great, eco-friendly way to traverse the country and you'll be rewarded with a saddle's-eye view of the landscape as it peaks and troughs across the Borders, Central Belt and Highlands. It even skirts the city centres of Edinburgh and Glasgow. Some of the northerly sections can be challenging, but each stretch is colour-coded for difficulty via the MTB Trail Grading System so there are no nasty surprises.

SMOO CAVE

A mile east of Durness is Smoo Cave, a gaping hole in a limestone cliff created by the sea and a small burn. Tucked at the end of a narrow cove, the main chamber is accessible via steps. The rock formations are quite impressive, and if the weather behaves you can take a fantastic 20-minute tour that is partly by rubber dinghy into two further caverns; after heavy rain a waterfall cascades through the middle. Nearby, the white sands of Balnakeil Bay are stunning in any weather, but especially spectacular when sunny days turn the sea a Mediterranean turquoise. A path winds through the dunes behind to Faraid Head – fine views east to Loch Eriboll and west to Cape Wrath make this circuit (3–4hr) the best in the area. While here, drop by the Balnakeil Craft Village, a hippie commune borne out of a disused 1970s military camp.

After heavy rain, a waterfall cascades through the cave

Sango Sands

Smoo Cave was created by the sea and a small burn

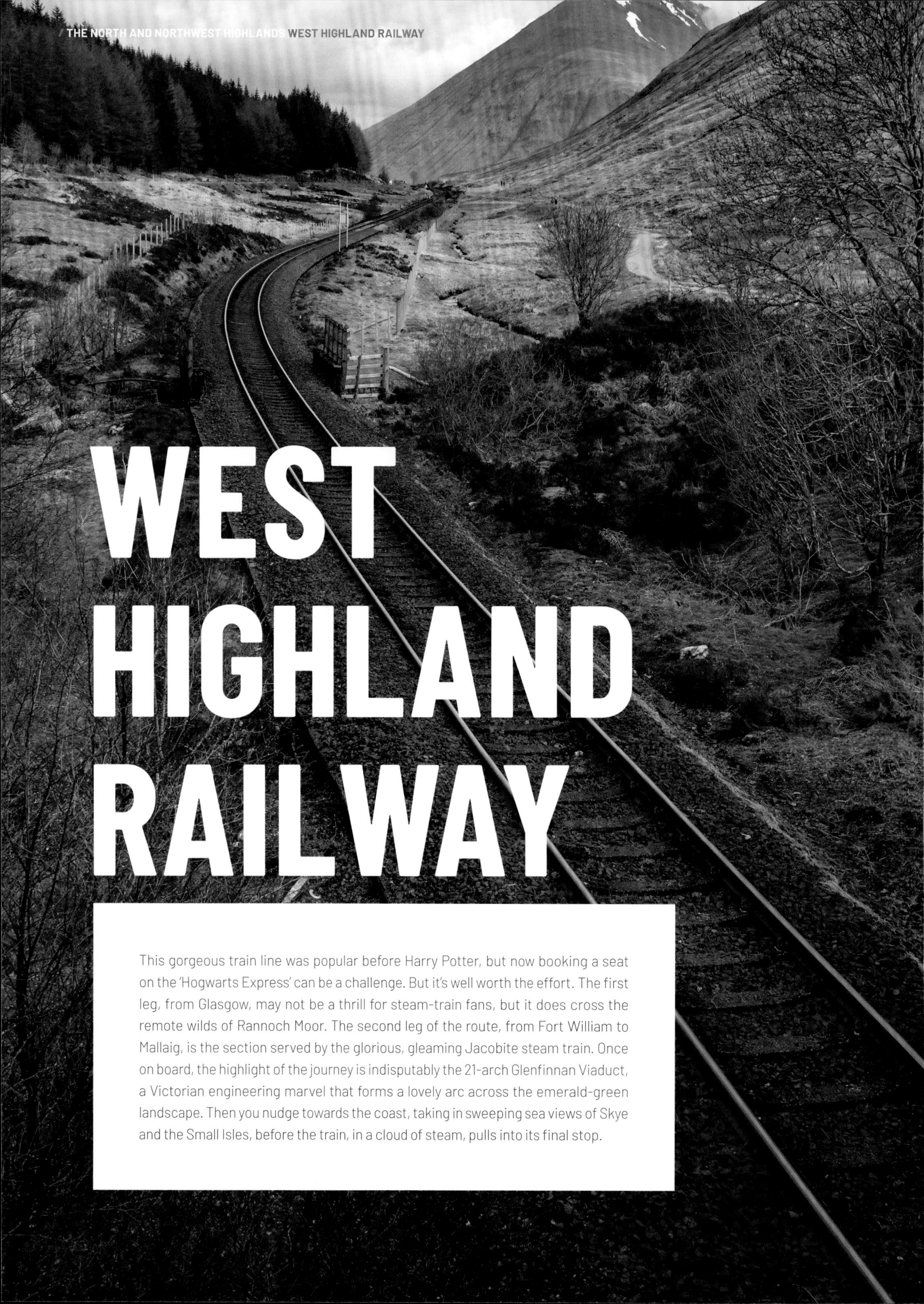

WEST HIGHLAND RAILWAY

This gorgeous train line was popular before Harry Potter, but now booking a seat on the 'Hogwarts Express' can be a challenge. But it's well worth the effort. The first leg, from Glasgow, may not be a thrill for steam-train fans, but it does cross the remote wilds of Rannoch Moor. The second leg of the route, from Fort William to Mallaig, is the section served by the glorious, gleaming Jacobite steam train. Once on board, the highlight of the journey is indisputably the 21-arch Glenfinnan Viaduct, a Victorian engineering marvel that forms a lovely arc across the emerald-green landscape. Then you nudge towards the coast, taking in sweeping sea views of Skye and the Small Isles, before the train, in a cloud of steam, pulls into its final stop.

Crossing Loch Awe

Jacobite steam train driver

The Jacobite steaming through Corpach

The infamous Glenfinnan Viaduct

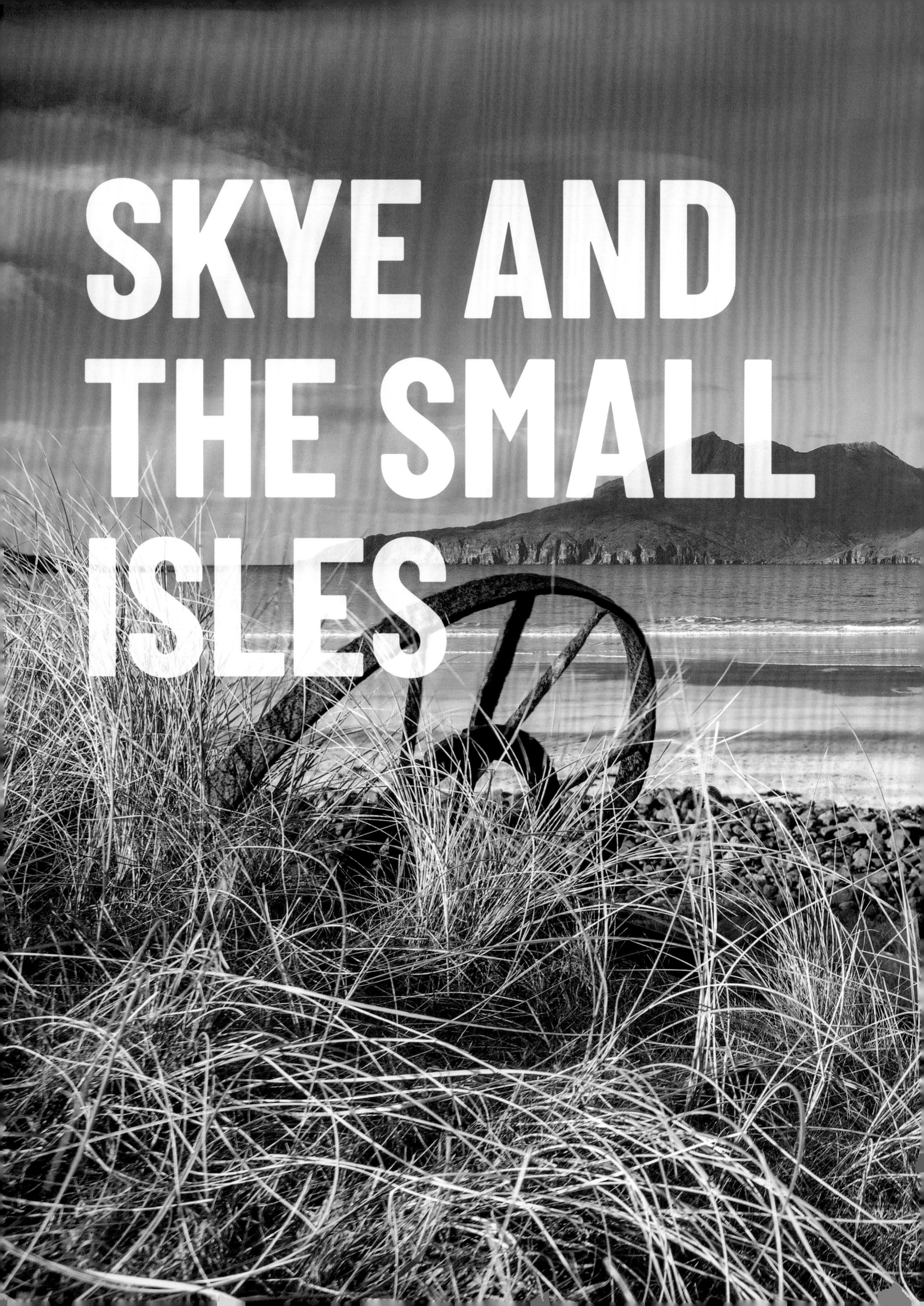

SKYE AND THE SMALL ISLES

THE CUILLIN

Sculpted by glaciers some 60 million years ago, The Cuillin was once a colossal volcano. Today, when the spectacular peaks aren't cloaked in mist, they dominate the Isle of Skye. Home to all the Munros on the island, the razor-edge mountain range includes the Black Cuillin, so-called for the colour of their coarse-grained jagged gabbro, and the gentler, rounded Red Cuillin, with picturesque Glen Sligachan between the two. Accessible viewpoints include Glenbrittle Campsite & Café, Sligachan village and the jaw-dropping boat trip from Elgol to Loch Coruisk. Hillwalkers and technical climbers get a lot closer to the action. Though none of the Munros are easily bagged, Bruach na Frìthe (3143ft), accessed via the Fairy Pools near Glenbrittle and Sgurr a' Fionn Choire, is the most straightforward. Not surprisingly, the menacing-sounding Inaccessible Pinnacle atop Sgùrr Dearg is generally considered the toughest.

The Cuillin was sculpted by glaciers some 60 million years ago

The Black Cullin, so-called for the colour of their coarse-grained gabbro

Hiking the range

An Sgùrr

EIGG

Eigg – which measures just five miles by three – does little to conceal its volcanic origins. It is made of a basalt plateau, and a great stump of pitchstone lava, known as An Sgùrr, rises in the south. Geology aside, Eigg has an appealingly strong sense of community among its 100-odd residents. This was given a boost in 1997 when they (alongside the Scottish Wildlife Trust) pulled off the first buyout of a Highlands estate, thereby ending Eigg's unhappy history of private ownership. The anniversary is celebrated with an all-night ceilidh on the weekend nearest June 12. Its other world-first is that its electricity grid is powered entirely by renewable sources. For visitors, the allure lies in scenic hikes, superb sea views and atmospheric crofting ruins. At low tide, scramble along the shore into Cathedral Cave or Massacre Cave (Uamh Fhraing), where all but one of Eigg's 396 inhabitants died in 1577, suffocated by the MacLeods of Skye, who lit a fire in the cave mouth.

The rock pools are filled with crystal-clear mountain spring water

Wildflowers flank the pools

Hiking past the Fairy Pools

One of Britain's most celebrated wild swimming destinations

FAIRY POOLS

One route into the mighty Cuillin is from Glenbrittle on the west side. The valley edges the most spectacular peaks, a semicircle of mountains which ring Loch Coruisk, before it runs to a beach at Loch Brittle. One of the least demanding walks is a five-mile round trip (3hr) from Glenbrittle campsite up Coire Làgan to a lochan squeezed among stern rock faces. An equally good reason to come is the Fairy Pools, one of Britain's most celebrated wild swimming destinations. There is no denying their beauty: sculpted rock pools filled with crystal-clear mountain spring water fed by a series of waterfalls. The scenery is superb as the river tumbles beneath peaks – the downside is icy water temperature of ten degrees Celsius at best, and its popularity is such that in summer months tailbacks of cars have been known to extend for miles along the single-track road. The pools are signposted from Glumagan Na Sithichean car park, five miles from the Glenbrittle turn. The largest waterfall is a 2.4km walk from the car park, or continue on to discover a string of smaller pools.

Tracing the mountain streams that feed the Fairy Pools

MUCK

Seen from southern Skye or the west coast of the Highlands, the Small Isles – Rùm, Eigg, Muck and dinky Canna – lie scattered in a silver-grey sea like a siren call to adventure. Barely two miles long, Muck is the smallest and most southerly of the archipelago. Its name derives from *muc*, the Gaelic for "pig" (or possibly *muc mara*, "sea pig" or porpoise, which are plentiful), and has long caused embarrassment to lairds – they preferred to call it the "Isle of Monk" because it briefly belonged to the medieval church. Port Mór is the hub of all activity, where just about all of the thirty or so residents live – a tenth of the 320 of the early 1800s. A mile-long road connects Port Mór with the island's main farm, Gallanach, which overlooks rocky skerries. The nicest sandy beach is Camas na Cairidh, to the east of Gallanach. For a stiffer challenge, Beinn Airein is worth climbing, despite being only 450ft above sea level, for a 360-degree panorama of surrounding islands from its summit. You can wild camp on the island or hole up in the Isle of Muck bunkhouse.

The Oyster Shed serves the freshest seafood on Skye

Oysters: the farm shop's raison d'être

Freshly caught seafood is sold that day

Grab a picnic bench for views across Loch Harport

The team even smoke their own salmon, oysters and shellfish

THE OYSTER SHED

Skye is the culinary capital of Scotland, luring globetrotting gourmands to the island. Whether you opt for silver service at Kinloch Lodge, French-influenced cuisine at Michelin-starred Loch Bay, cosy seafront dining at The Ferry Inn or dining in the kitchen at The Three Chimneys, you'll be in for a foodie treat. One of the forerunners of the gourmand scene, The Oyster Shed is an artisanal farm shop in Carbost, serving the freshest, best-value seafood you'll find anywhere on Skye. They now even smoke their own salmon, oysters and shellfish. Standouts include lobster tail in garlic butter and chips or hot smoked trout and chips. Take away or eat on the picnic benches overlooking Loch Harport. Combine a visit with the Talisker Distillery next door to wash down your lunch with a wee dram.

Rùm's highest mountain, Askival

Kinloch Castle

Visitors are permitted to wild camp on Rùm

White-tailed sea eagle

Rùm at sunrise

RÙM

After almost a century as the "Forbidden Isle" – the exclusive sporting estate of self-made Lancastrian industrialists the Bulloughs – Rùm has opened up. Many come to hike the eight-mile Rùm Cuillin Ridge Walk, tracking a crown of peaks that are modest by Skye's standards – the summit of Askival is only 2663ft – but every bit as impressive in looks. The island is renowned for its Manx shearwaters, which nest in burrows on high peaks. The best beach is Kilmory in the north, a flattish 10-mile walk on tracks through Kinloch then Kilmory glens. Most day-trippers to Rùm head straight for Kinloch Castle, a squat, red-sandstone edifice with decadent Edwardian interiors. It's also appealingly bonkers, packed with technical gizmos accumulated by Sir George Bullough (1870–1939), the spendthrift son of self-made millionaire, Sir John Bullough. Visitors are permitted to wild camp, or take your pick from two simple bothies, a campsite, one bunkhouse or the island's first B&B.

SLEAT

The Sleat peninsula is unlike almost anywhere else on the Isle of Skye. An uncharacteristically fertile area, this southern corner of the island has been branded "The Garden of Skye". The main attraction is the Armadale Castle estate, but in 2017, the Talisker Distillery at Torabhaig opened and tours and whisky tastings have since proved a hit. Scotland's most-touted island is the last place you'd expect to find a secret backcountry experience, yet look hard enough and Skye's Atlantic-facing sea lochs and islands remain a blank space for stand-up paddle boarding and sea-kayaking adventures. Set off from the beach at Ord across Loch Eishort, paddle to Coral Island, and then complete a wild camping circuit on Elgol by finishing back across the strait at Tokavaig. For a long day's paddle, embark from Armadale Castle to the isle of Ornsay, where you can splurge on a Michelin-starred dinner at Kinloch Lodge overlooking the Sound of Sleat.

Kinloch Lodge

Michelin-starred cuisine at Kinloch Lodge

Torabhaig Distillery

Armadale Castle

River Rha near Uig

Bride's Veil Waterfall near the Old Man of Storr

Fairy Glen

The ruins of Duntulm Castle

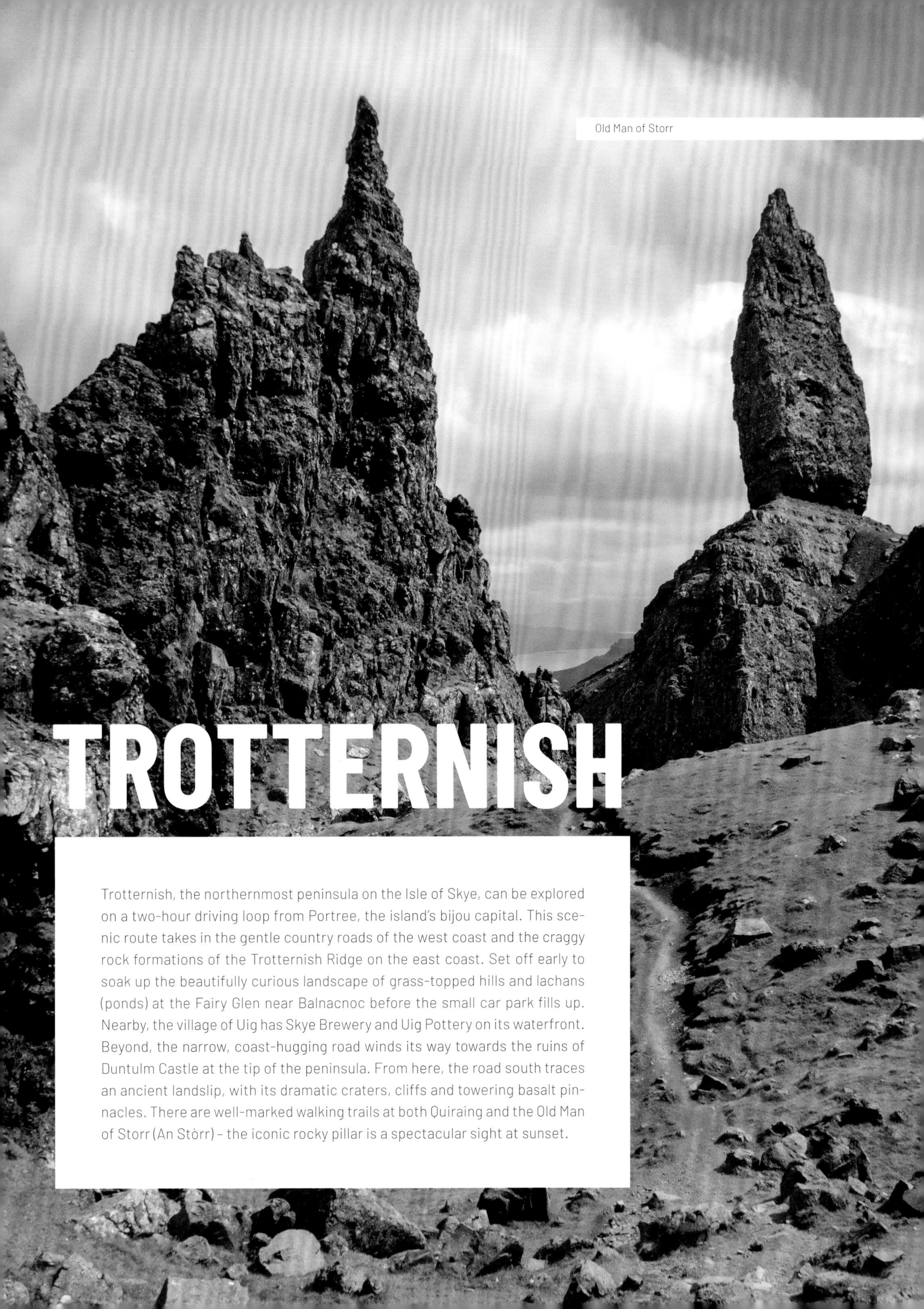

Old Man of Storr

TROTTERNISH

Trotternish, the northernmost peninsula on the Isle of Skye, can be explored on a two-hour driving loop from Portree, the island's bijou capital. This scenic route takes in the gentle country roads of the west coast and the craggy rock formations of the Trotternish Ridge on the east coast. Set off early to soak up the beautifully curious landscape of grass-topped hills and lachans (ponds) at the Fairy Glen near Balnacnoc before the small car park fills up. Nearby, the village of Uig has Skye Brewery and Uig Pottery on its waterfront. Beyond, the narrow, coast-hugging road winds its way towards the ruins of Duntulm Castle at the tip of the peninsula. From here, the road south traces an ancient landslip, with its dramatic craters, cliffs and towering basalt pinnacles. There are well-marked walking trails at both Quiraing and the Old Man of Storr (An Stòrr) – the iconic rocky pillar is a spectacular sight at sunset.

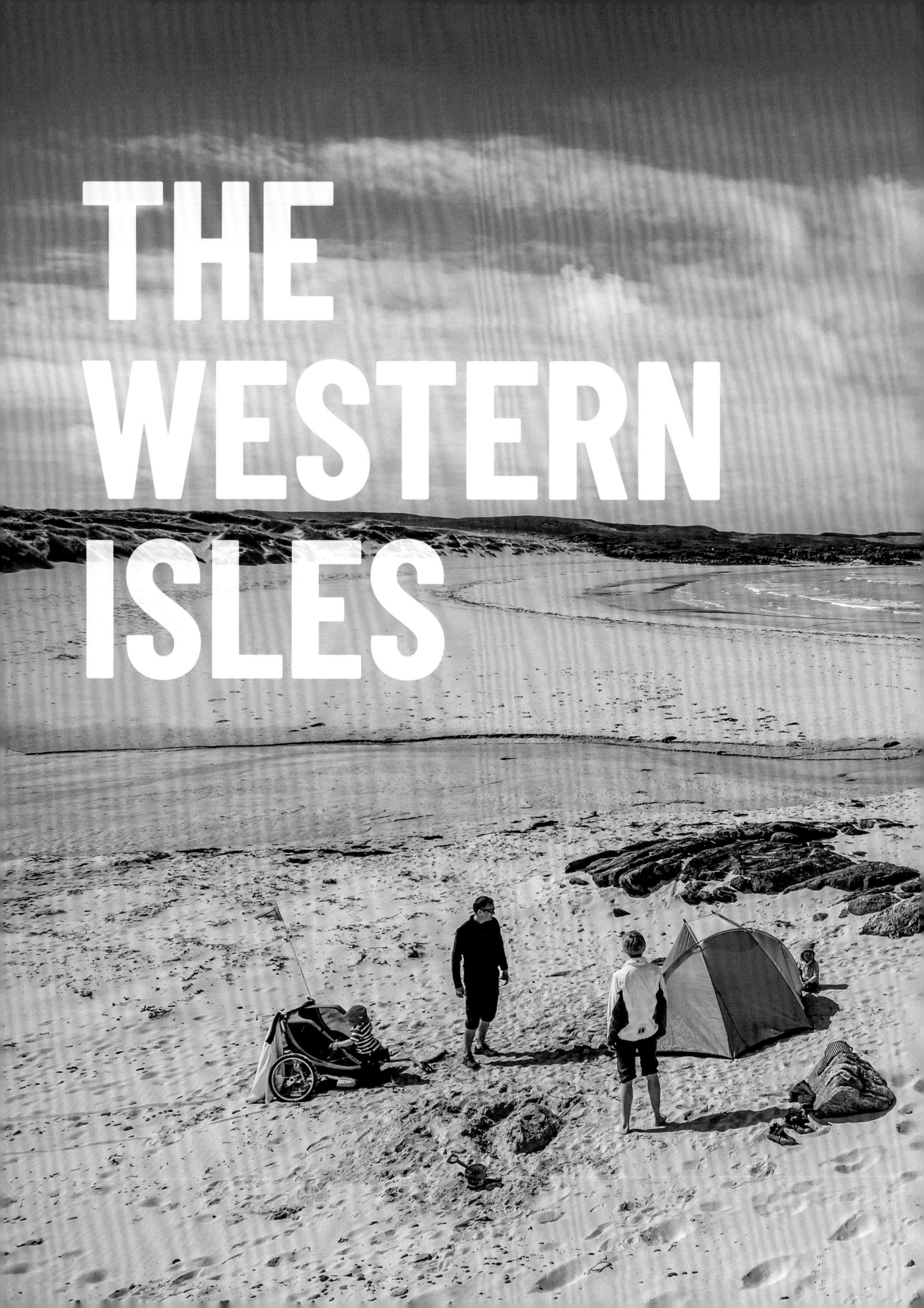
THE
WESTERN
ISLES

BARRA

Four miles wide and eight long, Barra is the Western Isles in miniature: sandy beaches, mountains of Lewisian gneiss – the oldest rock in Britain – prehistoric ruins and a Gaelic culture. A kind of feudal island state, it was ruled over for centuries by the MacNeils. Unfortunately, the family sold the island in 1838 to Colonel Gordon of Cluny, who deemed the starving crofters "redundant" and offered to turn Barra into a state penal colony. The government declined, so the colonel proceeded with some of the cruellest forced Clearances in the Hebrides. In 1937, the 45th chief of the MacNeil clan bought back most of the island, and in 2003 the estate was gifted to the Scottish government. At the island's southern tip, Castlebay – as its name suggests – has a castle in its bay: the picturesque medieval islet-fortress of Caisteal Chiosmuil, or Kisimul Castle, ancestral home of the MacNeil clan. To the west are the fine sandy beaches of Halaman Bay and Allasdale (Allathasdal), while rocky bays bite into the east coast. Further north, Barra is squeezed between two sandy bays: one of which – Tràigh Mhòr, or Cockle Strand – is also used as the island's airport, with planes landing on and taking off from the sandy runway at low tide.

Kisimul Castle

A detail of Kisimul Castle, Castlebay

Barra Airport, Traigh Mhor Beach

Sea Kayaking with Clearwater Paddling

Traigh Iar Beach in Harris

The Calanais Standing Stones predate England's Stonehenge

The Lewis Chessmen in Lews Castle Museum

The road to Leverburgh in Harris

The beach at Luskentyre, Isle of Harris

LEWIS AND HARRIS

The most northerly of the Outer Hebrides (Western Isles), Lewis and Harris is, despite the name, just one island. Lewis (Leodhas) in the north is home to the Hebrides' main town of Stornaway and the Museum nan Eilean, with its famous twelfth-century chess pieces carved in Norway, as well as the Calanais Standing Stones that predate England's Stonehenge. Culture aside, most people visit Lewis and Harris for the dramatic landscapes, empty beaches, wild moorland and scenic lochs. The ruggedly beautiful mountains of North Harris are latticed with peaceful trails, and beyond tiny Tarbert, which links North and South Harris, it's all machair-strewn grassy plains and pearly white shell beaches. Stunning Luskentyre Beach, with its jewel-blue sea and rolling dunes, is unmissable.

ST KILDA

Britain's westernmost island chain is the St Kilda archipelago, forty miles from North Uist. Dominated by Britain's highest cliffs and sea stacks, Hirta, the main island, was occupied until 1930 when the last 36 Gaelic-speaking inhabitants were evacuated at their own request. The Marquess of Bute then bought the island to protect the millions of nesting seabirds. In 1957, having allowed the army to build a missile-tracking radar station here linked to South Uist, the marquess bequeathed the island to the National Trust for Scotland (NTS). St Kilda is one of only two-dozen Unesco World Heritage Sites with a dual status reflecting its natural and cultural significance. Despite its inaccessibility, several thousand visitors make it out here each year; if you get to land, you can see the museum, send a postcard and take in the glorious views. Between May and August, the NTS organizes volunteer parties to restore and maintain the old buildings or take part in archeological digs.

Pobull Fhinn Stone Circle

Tràigh-Stir, one of North Uist's finest beaches

The "drowned landscape" of North Uist

Scolpaig Tower, a Georgian folly

NORTH UIST

Compared to the mountainous scenery of Harris, North Uist – seventeen miles long and thirteen miles wide – is much flatter than its popular neighbour. Over half the surface area is covered by water, creating a distinctive peaty-brown lochan-studded "drowned landscape". Most visitors come here for the trout- and salmon-fishing and the deerstalking, all of which (along with poaching) are critical to the survival of the island's economy. Others come for the smattering of prehistoric sites, the birds, the otters, or the sheer peace of this windy isle and the solitude of North Uist's vast sandy beaches, which extend – almost without interruption – along the north and west coasts. Base yourself in sleepy Lochmaddy to explore the cluster of prehistoric sites nearby. The only other thing to keep you in the port town is Taigh Chearsabhagh, a converted eighteenth-century merchant's house, now home to a community arts centre, with an airy café, shop and excellent museum, which puts on some worthwhile exhibitions.

Lochmaddy village

SOUTH UIST

South Uist is the largest and most varied of the southern chain of islands. The west coast boasts some of the region's finest machair and beaches – a necklace of gold and grey sand strung twenty miles from one end to the other – while the east coast features a ridge of high mountains rising to 2034ft at Beinn Mhòr. One of the best places to reach the sandy shoreline is at Howmore (Tobha Mòr), a pretty little crofting settlement with a number of restored houses, many still thatched, including one distinctively roofed in brown heather. It's an easy walk from the village church across the flower-strewn machair to the gorgeous beach. In among the crofts are the shattered, lichen-encrusted remains of no fewer than four medieval churches and chapels, and a burial ground now harbouring just a few scattered graves.

Machair Way, a walking route at Bornish

Loch Druidibeg National Nature Reserve

South Uist boasts some of the region's finest beaches

Eriskay ponies, a native breed roaming near Lochboisdale

ORKNEY AND SHETLAND

SWAN

FAIR ISLE

Marooned in the sea halfway between Shetland and Orkney, Fair Isle is very different from both. The weather reflects its isolated position: you can almost guarantee that it'll be windy, though if you're lucky your visit might coincide with fine weather - what the islanders call "a given day". The magical little island is bookended by a pair of a lighthouses, with a world-famous bird observatory in the middle. Fair Isle's population tumbled from 400 to 44 by the 1950s, at which point evacuation was seriously considered. The laird, George Waterston, who'd set up a bird observatory in 1948, passed it into the care of the National Trust for Scotland in 1954 and rejuvenation began. Today, Fair Isle supports a community of around sixty. The north end of the island rises like a wall, while the Sheep Rock, a sculpted stack of rock and grass on the east side, is another dramatic feature. Fair Isle's two lighthouses, one at either end of the island, are both designed by the Stevenson family and were erected in 1892 - the South Lighthouse can be visited by appointment.

Fair Isle is marooned in the sea between Shetland and Orkney

Atlantic puffin silhouetted at sunset on Fair Isle

North Lighthouse

Great skua seabird

Guillemots nesting in the cliffs

Northern gannet

Cliffs plunge 500ft into the sea at the eastern tip of Noss

Noss has the distinctive outline of a half-sunk ocean liner

ISLE OF NOSS

Appropriately enough for an island that slopes gently into the sea at its western end, and plunges vertically 500ft at its eastern end, Noss has the dramatic and distinctive outline of a half-sunk ocean liner, while its name means "a point of rock". Inhabited until World War II, it's now a nature reserve and sheep farm, managed by Scottish Natural Heritage, who operate a RIB ferry from Bressay. An old farmhouse contains a small visitor centre, where the warden will give you a quick briefing and a free map. Nearby is a sandy beach, while behind the *haa* (laird's house) is a Pony Pund, a square stone enclosure built for the breeding of Shetland ponies. The most memorable feature of Noss is its eastern sea cliffs, rising to a 500ft peak at Noup, home to vast colonies of cliff-nesting gannets, puffins, guillemots, shags, razorbills and fulmars: one of the highlights of Shetland. As Noss is only a mile or so wide, it's easy enough to walk to the sea cliffs and back, but make sure you keep close to the coast, since otherwise the great *skuas* (locally known as "bonxies") may well dive-bomb you.

JARLSHOF

Of all the archeological sites in Shetland, Jarlshof is the largest and most impressive. What makes Jarlshof so amazing is the fact that you can walk right into a house built 1600 years ago, which is still intact to above head height. The name - misleading, as it is not primarily a Viking site - was coined by Sir Walter Scott, who used the ruins of the Old House in his novel *The Pirate*. However, it was only at the end of the nineteenth century that the Bronze Age, Iron Age and Viking settlements you see now were discovered, after a violent storm ripped off the top layer of turf. Only half of the original broch survives, and its courtyard is now an Iron Age aisled roundhouse, with stone piers. Inland lies the maze of grass-topped foundations marking out the Viking longhouses, from the ninth century AD. Towering over the whole complex are the ruins of the laird's house, built by Robert Stewart, Earl of Orkney and Lord of Shetland, in the late sixteenth century, and the Old House of Sumburgh, built by his son, Earl Patrick.

Sunset from North Ronaldsay Lighthouse

Looking out to sea from the foghorn

North Ronaldsay knitwear

North Ronaldsay sheep are noted for their seaweed diet

North Ronaldsay has an outpost atmosphere, brought about by its extreme isolation

NORTH RONALDSAY

North Ronaldsay – or "North Ron" as it's fondly known – is Orkney's most northerly island, with a population of around fifty. Separated from Sanday by some treacherous waters, it has an outpost atmosphere, brought about by its extreme isolation. Measuring just three miles by one, and rising only 66ft above sea level, the only features to interrupt the flat horizon are Holland House – built by the Traill family, who bought the island in 1727 – and a pair of lighthouses at Dennis Head. The island's most frequent visitors are ornithologists, who come to clock the rare migrants that land here briefly on their spring and autumn migrations. The island has two lighthouses: the attractive, stone-built Old Beacon was first lit in 1789, but the lantern was replaced by the current huge bauble of masonry in 1809. The New Lighthouse, designed by Alan Stevenson in 1854 just to the north, is Britain's tallest land-based lighthouse, at over 100ft. Climb the 176 steps to the top of the lighthouse and admire the view – on a clear day you can see Fair Isle, and even Shetland.

Sand dunes concealed the magical cluster of stone houses for centuries

Narrow passageways connect the houses

Dating back 5000 years, the Neolithic houses are incredibly well preserved

Skara Brae is older than Stonehenge and the Great Pyramids

SKARA BRAE

Lots of great stories start with a storm, and the discovery of the Neolithic homes at Skara Brae was thanks to an 1850 squall that blew away the sand dunes that for centuries had hidden this magical cluster of stone houses. Older than Stonehenge or the Great Pyramids, Skara Brae is a mesmerizing Neolithic settlement, crammed with domestic detail. Dating back 5000 years, the houses are incredibly well preserved, with narrow connecting passageways which would once have been covered with turf. Each home consists of a single living room, where stone cupboards, beds, boxes and fireplaces all survive to give a miraculous sense of early domestic life. It's thought that the inhabitants were some of Britain's earliest farmers: they grew wheat crops and raised pigs, sheep and cows. No weapons were found, indicating that life was peaceful here; what archeologists did discover were needles, jewellery, ceramics, buttons and dice, all suggestive of a creative, settled community.

Archeologists unearthed signs of a creative, settled community

SUMBURGH HEAD

Shetland's South Mainland is a long, thin finger of land, only three or four miles wide but 25 miles long, ending dramatically in Sumburgh Head (262ft). The road up to the vertical cliffs is the perfect site for watching nesting seabirds such as kittiwakes, fulmars, shags, razorbills and guillemots, as well as gannets nosediving for fish. This is also the easiest place in Shetland to get close to puffins: during the nesting season (May to early Aug), you simply need to look over the wall as you enter the lighthouse complex to see them in their burrows a few yards below with beaks full of sand eels. Visit the clifftop lighthouse, built by Robert Stevenson in 1821, and explore some of the outbuildings, including the reconstructed WWII secret radar hut which helped protect the Royal Navy anchored in Scapa Flow. After roaming the complex, settle down and enjoy the sea views from the lighthouse's café.

Sumburgh Head is the easiest place in Shetland to get close to puffins

Foghorn at the lighthouse

Sea views from Sumburgh Head

Clifftop lighthouse

INDEX

THE UNIVERSITY CAFÉ
TEAS · COFFEES
take Away
ICES · SANDWICHES
EST 1918
A&P VERRECCHIA
TEL 0141 -339-5217

Otters
rossing

ADIESWEAR
44
40
20
HARRY
SEND
HELP!

CONTRIBUTORS

Greg Dickinson
Brendan Griffin
Rob Humphreys
Norm Longley
Rachel Mills
Keith Munro
Joanna Reeves
Helena Smith

PHOTO CREDITS

Alamy 198, 206
Alexander Baxter 140TR, 140BR, 140BL
Alistair Edwards 187TL
Andrew Downie/Edinburgh Festival Fringe Society 14BR
Andrew Maccoll/Shutterstock 184/185
Ardoch Estate Loch Lomond 112/113
Conde Nast Traveller/www.jamesbedford.com 187TR
Courtesy of Jupiter Artland 22, 23TR, 23BR, 23TL, 23TR
Cycling UK/ Max Darkins 190/191
DC Thomson & Co Ltd 163TR
Eilean Shona 187BR
Fife Council/Damian Shields 130, 131TL, 131TR, 131BR, 131BL
FLPA/David Hosking/Shutterstock 95BR
FLPA/Wayne Hutchinson/Shutterstock 104, 105T
Getty Images 56BL, 196/197
Glasgow Life 8/9T, 70/71, 73TR, 76/77, 78, 79TL, 79TR, 79BR, 79BL, 82, 83TR, 83BR, 83BL, 83TL, 241TR
Hebridean Whale & Dolphin Trust 90/91
Helen Cathcart 211TR
Horst Friedrichs 211BL
Hufton + Crow Photography 163BR
Ian Rutherford/Shutterstock 95TL
Inverlonan Estates 92TL, 92TR, 92BL, 92BR, 93
iStockphoto 199BL
ITV/Shutterstock 50TR, 50BR, 50TL
Jane Barlow/Shutterstock 105BR
Jonathan Perugia/Shutterstock 126TL
Karma Lake of Menteith 118TR
Keith Hunter Photography 31
Kinloch Lodge 211TR
Kirsty Anderson 74BL, 74TL, 75
Liam Jones 186, 187BL
Lisa Flemming 30BR, 30TL
Lynn Bowser/Argaty Red Kites 115TL, 115BR, 115BL
Marine & Lawn Hotels 134, 135TR, 135BR, 135BL, 135TL
Markus Keller/imageBROKER/Shutterstock 192
Mockford & Bonetti/Apa Publications 64
Moor of Rannoch Restaurant & Rooms 148/149
Mount Stewart 100
National Galleries of Scotland/Keith Hunter Photography 30BL
National Museums Scotland 26
NorthLink Ferries 229T
PA Archive/PA Images 29, 50BL, 51
Peter McNally 174TL, 174BL
Philip Dunn/Shutterstock 182/183
Rex/Shutterstock 68TR
Richard Elliot/VisitScotland 219
Robert Perry/EPA-EFE/Shutterstock 154BL
ScotRail 195TL
Scottish National Gallery of Modern Art 30TR
SG CIC Glasgow Museums Collections 73TL
Shutterstock 10/11, 13TL, 13TR, 13BR, 13BL, 14TR, 14BL, 18TL, 18TR, 18BL, 18BR, 19, 20/21, 25BR, 25BL, 27BR, 28TR, 28BL, 36TL, 36BR, 37, 41TL, 42/43, 46TL, 46BL, 49TR, 62TL, 63, 67TR, 67BR, 67TL, 72, 86, 87BR, 88TL, 94, 95TR, 95BL, 96, 97TR, 97BR, 97BL, 97TL, 102TR, 102BR, 102BL, 102TL, 103, 106TL, 106TR, 106BL, 106BR, 107, 108, 109T, 109BL, 109BR, 110/111, 114, 115TR, 118BL, 118TL, 120, 122TL, 123, 126TR, 126BL, 126BR, 127, 129, 154TR, 155, 161T, 161BL, 178, 179TL, 179TR, 179BR, 179BL, 180TR, 180BR, 180BL, 181, 188, 189TL, 189TR, 189BL, 193T, 193BL, 193BR, 194, 195TR, 195BR, 195BL, 199BR, 202TR, 202BR, 202BL, 202TL, 203, 204/205, 207BR, 208TL, 208TR, 208BR, 208BL, 209, 210, 211BR, 212TL, 212TR, 212BR, 212BL, 213, 220/221, 228, 229BL, 229BR, 230TL, 230BR, 230BL, 230TR, 232/233, 236TR, 236BR, 236BL, 237, 239TL, 239TR, 239BL
Sim Canetty-Clarke 159T, 159BL, 159BR
South of Scotland Destination Alliance/ Duncan Ireland 32/33, 39TL, 39BL, 55T
Spitfire Espresso 74TR, 74BR
The Gleneagles Hotel 144, 145T, 145BL, 145BR
The Glenturret 146, 147TL, 147BR, 147BL
The Oyster Shed 207TR, 207BL, 207TR
The Prince's Foundation/Dumfries House 68TL, 69BR
Vicky Brock 231
VisitScotland 238, 241TL
VisitScotland/Airborne Lens 6/7, 80TL
VisitScotland/Damian Shields 9, 44/45, 46TR, 46BR, 47, 55BR, 58/59, 68BL, 69, 138/139, 174TR, 174BR, 175, 242TR, 245TR, 247TL
VisitScotland/David N Anderson 34, 35TL, 35TR, 35BR, 35BL, 48, 49BL
VisitScotland/Ian Rutherford 39BR, 41TR
VisitScotland/Jakub Iwanicki 2/3, 164/165, 167TL, 244/245T
VisitScotland/John Duncan 200/201
VisitScotland/Kenny Lam 8B, 8TL, 12, 14TL, 15, 16/17, 24, 25TL, 27TL, 27TR, 27BR, 28TL, 28BR, 36TR, 36BL, 38, 40, 41BR, 41BL, 54, 55BL, 56TL, 56BR, 57, 60/61, 62TR, 62BR, 65T, 65BR, 73BR, 73BL, 80TR, 80BR, 80BL, 81, 87T, 87BL, 101T, 101BL, 101BR, 116/117, 119, 121TL, 121TR, 121BR, 121BL, 122TR, 122BR, 122BL, 128TR, 128BR, 128BL, 128TL, 132, 133T, 133BL, 133BR, 136TR, 136BR, 136BL, 137, 142TL, 142TR, 142BL, 142BR, 143, 147TR, 153TL, 153TR, 154TL, 154BR, 156/157, 158, 160, 162, 163TL, 163BL, 166, 167TR, 167BR, 167BL, 168/169, 170BR, 170BL, 171, 172, 173T, 173BR, 176/177, 180TL, 199T, 218TR, 218BL, 236TL, 242TL, 242C, 242B, 247TR, 247B
VisitScotland/Luigi Di Pasquale 173BL, 241BR, 244/245B
VisitScotland/Paul Tomkins 49TL, 49BR, 56TR, 62BL, 65BL, 66, 67BL, 84/85, 88TR, 88BR, 88BL, 89, 98TL, 98TR, 98BR, 98BL, 99, 105BL, 118BR, 124/125, 140TL, 141, 150/151, 161BR, 170TR, 170TL, 189BR, 214/215, 216, 217TL, 217TR, 217BR, 217BL, 218TL, 218BR, 222TR, 222BR, 222BL, 222TL, 223, 224, 225TL, 225TR, 225BR, 225BL, 226/227, 234TR, 234BR, 234TL, 234BL, 235, 239BR, 241BL, 244BL
VisitScotland/PRImaging 39TR, 52/53, 245BR
VisitScotland/Stuart Brunton 136TL
Vistit Scotland/Visit Aberdeenshire 152, 153BR, 153BL

Cover **Sum Glen** Shutterstock